There was

a President

Ridge Press ⬛ Random House, New York

Prepared and produced by ☀ The Ridge Press, Inc., New York

Published in New York by Random House, Inc.

Original, unillustrated edition published as "Seventy Hours and Thirty Minutes"

Text © Copyright 1966 by National Broadcasting Company, Inc.

© Copyright 1966 by Random House, Inc. and Ridge Press, Inc.

Photographic Research: Dell Byrne Fischer

Library of Congress Catalogue Card Number 66-28547

Printed in the United States of America

1:45:03 pm
NBC NEWS
BULLETIN
(WNBC-TV
ONLY)

ANNOUNCER (voice over): President Kennedy was shot at in Dallas, Texas, today. Blood was seen on the President's head as they rushed him to the hospital. Mrs. Kennedy was heard to exclaim, "Oh, no."

STATION TIME INTERRUPTED.

1:46:45 pm
NBC NEWS
BULLETIN
(NETWORK)

ANNOUNCER (voice over): President Kennedy and Gov. John Connally of Texas were cut down by an assassin's bullet in downtown Dallas and were rushed to an emergency room at Parkland Hospital. The President's limp body was seen cradled in the arms of his wife. There is no information at present on his condition.

CONTINUOUS COVERAGE BEGINS.
ALL REGULAR PROGRAMS CANCELED.

1:53:12 pm
NEW YORK

BILL RYAN: Bullet wounds were clearly visible on Gov. Connally's chest; blood was visible on the President's head. He was lying flat on the floor of the Presidential car. No answer was given reporters as to whether the President is dead. He has been wounded, and we do not know his condition.

CHET HUNTLEY: Circuits are all tied up, but we know that the President has been shot in a motorcade in Dallas. Mrs. Kennedy, who was seated in the car next to her husband, leaped up and said, "Oh, no." At first the shots were thought to be fireworks.

RYAN: The White House has no word to give. Acting Press Secretary Malcolm Kilduff says he has no word at this time. All we know is that each man was wounded—no report on how serious.

HUNTLEY: No time for speculation.... This in from Dallas.... They are both still alive—both wounded by an assailant. It is not known if the Secret Service agents had a chance to return the assailant's gunfire. The President was slumped over face down in the back of the famed bubble-top car. The bubble-top was down. Rep. Albert Thomas of Texas has said the President is still alive, but his condition is very critical.

Friday, Nov. 22, 1963

RYAN: The Presidental motorcade was at a triple underpass on a Dallas freeway. A call has been sent out from Parkland Hospital for top surgical specialists and for a priest.

HUNTLEY: Special Presidential Assistant Kenneth O'Donnell gave no answer when asked if President Kennedy was dead. Blood was streaming from the President's head. Driving at high speed, the car took five minutes to get to the hospital. A man and woman were seen scrambling on the underpass.

Senator Ralph Yarborough

RYAN: When a Catholic is listed in critical condition, it is the usual procedure to summon a priest. The last word we have is that President Kennedy and Gov. Connally are still alive.

FRANK McGEE: speaks with NBC Newsman Robert MacNeil by telephone from Parkland Hospital, Dallas, where President Kennedy has been taken.

McGEE: MacNeil reports that the President is seriously wounded—this from Sen. Ralph Yarborough of Texas, who was with the President. The shots were fired while the motorcade was proceeding through downtown Dallas; Gov. Connally was also hit. Mrs. Kennedy, who was seated beside the President, was not hurt. The assassin is believed to have fired from a building overlooking the parade route. People fanned out and were asked if they saw anyone at a window. MacNeil says he was with the motorcade when the shooting occurred. When the shots rang out, people lay down and screamed. . . . A white man was seen in a window with a rifle.

RYAN: The President is in very critical condition.

HUNTLEY: The President is still in the emergency room. Gov. Connally has been taken to the operating room of Parkland Hospital.

2:15 pm
DALLAS, TEX.
(WBAP-TV)
CHARLES MURPHY: A time of controlled panic. Mrs. Kennedy was not injured. . . . A man

was seen in a window a block away from the freeway where President Kennedy's car passed by. The President's condition is critical, but to our knowledge, he is still alive. . . . A young man has been taken into custody, vehemently protesting his innocence—a young man in his early twenties, neatly dressed. . . . Two Roman Catholic priests were summoned to the room of President Kennedy. . . . The President has been given blood transfusions.

2:17 pm
NEW YORK

RYAN: A call has been issued for fresh blood—B-positive type.

2:19 pm
WASHINGTON, D.C.

DAVID BRINKLEY: Congress has recessed, and Congressmen have tuned to NBC for news of the President's condition. On the floor of the Senate, Sen. Edward Kennedy, the President's brother, was informed by Sen. Mike Mansfield that the President had been shot. The White House has no more information than we have. The stock exchange closed on word of the assassination attempt.

2:21 pm
DALLAS

TOM WHALEN conducts an interview with Jean Hill, an eyewitness to the shooting.

JEAN HILL: I heard two shots ring out. The President fell over, and then Mrs. Kennedy fell over him and shouted, "My God, he's been shot." The car speeded away, and I saw a man running back up the hill.

2:23 pm
NEW YORK

McGEE speaks by telephone with Robert MacNeil, in Dallas.

MacNEIL: Last rites of the Roman Catholic Church have been administered to President Kennedy. This does not necessarily mean that his condition is fatal. Vice President Lyndon B. Johnson walked into the hospital where the President is being treated. Mrs. Johnson said her husband is all right. She did not want to say anything about the President; she is in a state of shock. A blood transfusion is being prepared for President Kennedy. . . . Gov. Connally was shot just

Police remove clothes from hospital

Friday, Nov. 22, 1963

below the shoulder blades in back. He was reported as saying, "Take care of Nellie for me." Nellie is Mrs. Connally.

McGEE: A call has gone out for a neuro-surgeon, indicating damage to the President's head or spine. The President was reported as conscious while being taken to the hospital. One neurosurgeon has definitely arrived at the hospital.

RYAN reads an Associated Press report stating that the two priests said the President is dead of bullet wounds.

RYAN: The report is confirmed: The President is dead. This has been substantiated by Charles Murphy in Dallas.

2:36 pm
DALLAS
MacNEIL: The White House has announced that President Kennedy is dead. The President died approximately 25 minutes after the shooting took place. A priest emerged from the emergency room after giving last rites. . . . The Dallas police had set up a stringent protection force, anticipating demonstrations such as those which greeted Adlai Stevenson here a short while back. . . . The shots came from a building called the Texas School Book Depository.

RYAN: Vice President Lyndon B. Johnson has been taken into seclusion. He will succeed the late President Kennedy as President of the United States.

2:40 pm
WASHINGTON, D.C.
BRINKLEY: Vice President Johnson will be given the oath of office as soon as it can be managed. Anyone, even a Justice of the Peace, can administer the oath. Johnson will finish out the term of the late President to January, 1965. The U.S. Air Force has four jets on the ramp ready to take off for Texas from Washington, D.C. We assume Mr. Johnson will return to Washington immediately to take over his duties. When he left as Vice President, he turned over his duties as President of the Senate to Sen. Ted Kennedy.

During search for assassin

A reporter in the press gallery gave the news of the assassination to a page, who informed Sen. Kennedy. The Senate chaplain said a prayer. Cabinet members—Secretaries Rusk, Udall and others—were on their way to Japan, one hour out of Hawaii; they have now turned back. The Kennedy children are in Washington. Gov. Connally has been shot in the chest and wrist. A young man was picked up and is being questioned.

2:45 pm
NEW YORK HUNTLEY: The President was seen cradled in his wife's arms, and was reportedly unconscious at the hospital. The last rites of the Roman Catholic Church were administered by the Very Rev. Oscar L. Huber. Johnson's whereabouts are not known. The President lived only about an hour after the bullet cut him down. The announcement by the two priests brought sobs and outcries at the hospital. The shots came from the right rear and struck the President's head.

2:49 pm
DALLAS MURPHY: A car has been stopped at Fort Worth which may have some connection with the shooting. . . . A Dallas policeman has been shot to death two miles from the scene of the assassination. A suspect is now in custody.

2:50 pm
NEW YORK RYAN speaks by telephone with John Hoefan, an NBC sound man who was an eyewitness to the shooting. Hoefan reports that he was in the motorcade with the Presidential party. . . . A loud shot rang out; people ducked; men and women were screaming. . . . Hoefan says that Malcolm Kilduff of the Presidential news staff is keeping the network abreast of all developments.

MacNEIL (voice over from Dallas): The President's body will be sent to Washington, D.C., this afternoon.

MERRILL MUELLER: A man saw a gun in the window of a building as the President's car went beneath the underpass. . . . Gov. Connally is in satisfactory condition. . . . Mrs. Johnson was in another car with her husband. The

Johnsons are in seclusion.... This is the first assassination since William McKinley.

McGEE: John F. Kennedy was the third American President to be assassinated since Abraham Lincoln.

On Camera: The White House flag flying at half-staff.

2:56 pm
WHITE HOUSE

MARTIN AGRONSKY: No statements have been made as yet by any of the nation's leaders.... Sen. Hubert Humphrey was informed of the President's assassination while attending a luncheon at the Chilean Embassy in Washington. When told of the tragedy, Sen. Edward Kennedy very quietly laid down the gavel; he was substituting for Vice President Johnson as President of the Senate.... It is difficult to contemplate or to understand how such a young, vital man should now be dead, and in this fashion.

3:00 pm
NEW YORK

McGEE comments on President Kennedy's visit to New York City last week. He speaks with MacNeil on the telephone in Dallas.

MacNEIL: There was a good reaction to President Kennedy by the people of Dallas today. It was thought that right-wing conservatives might have given the President a bad reception, and there was a strong campaign by the police force to make sure that the name of Dallas would not be dragged in the mud by extremists.... The President's body will be placed in a bronze casket.... Men and women were lying on the ground to escape the bullets; there was the sound of wailing when it became clear what was happening. As far as we know, no one but President Kennedy and Gov. Connally were hit. The assassin fired the shots from a fourth floor window, 100 yards from the President's car. The President was struck in the right temple by the bullet. It is now an hour and a half since he was killed.... I was in the reporter's car, three cars behind the President. The President was seated. There were very few people on the street at that particular

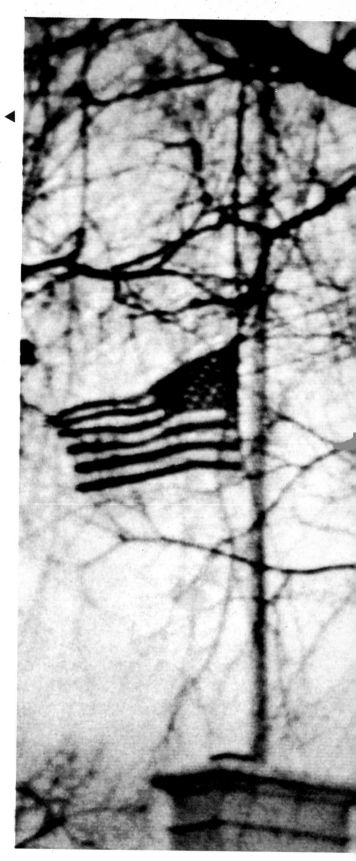

point in the motorcade. The Texas School Book Depository building is about eight floors high. With a high-powered rifle it would have been possible to hit the President at this distance. Vice President Lyndon B. Johnson—now President Johnson—was in the car immediately behind the President. He was not hurt.

3:10 pm
UNITED NATIONS
U THANT, UN Secretary General, calls President Kennedy's death "a loss to all mankind."

CARLOS SOSA RODRIGUEZ, President of the General Assembly, asks all to rise for one minute of silence.

On Camera: The members of the General Assembly, including U.S. Ambassador Adlai Stevenson. At the conclusion of the silent tribute, the session is adjourned.

3:12 pm
NEW YORK
RYAN: At no time has Mrs. Kennedy given way to hysteria.

3:13 pm
DALLAS
WHALEN: The weapon which was used to kill the President, and which wounded Gov. Connally, has been found in the Texas School Book Depository on the sixth floor—a British 303 rifle with a telescopic sight. Three empty cartridge cases were found beside the weapon. It appeared that whoever had occupied this sniper's nest had been here for some time.

Silent tribute at United Nations

3:15 pm
NEW YORK
CHARLES BREND (voice over from Dallas): I was 15 to 20 feet away from the President. I was holding my five-year-old son, and I told him to wave at the President as he passed by. The President waved back [Brend's voice breaks] and the next thing I knew a shot rang out and the President slumped down. I didn't see the man who did it; I will never forget it. I fell on the ground, and then I fell on my son to protect him for fear the lunatic would shoot anyone around.

McGEE: The sniper's nest has been found. It has been reported that a Dallas policeman and a Secret Service agent have been shot. A wanted car has been picked up, and a suspect. The body of President John F. Kennedy has been taken from Parkland Hospital. We assume it will be taken to the airport for return to Washington.

RYAN: George Reedy, assistant to Lyndon Johnson, is going to Washington. The President's father and mother, Mr. and Mrs. Joseph Kennedy, have been informed that their son has been wounded in Dallas. Gov. John Connally has been operated on, and reports indicate he is in as good condition as can be expected. European nations have been informed of the news; the Vatican has received word of the President's death. Tass, the Russian news agency, carried an announcement saying, "It has been officially announced that President Kennedy is dead after being shot by a man of the extreme right-wing element." A white man in his early twenties has been taken into custody for the shooting of a Dallas policeman in the Riverside section of Fort Worth.... We have conflicting reports on the weapon used to murder the President. Reports now indicate that a German Mauser has been found. Three bullets were used—one was still in the gun. The gun had a telescopic sight.

McGEE: Vice President Lyndon B. Johnson was sped to the hospital. Sen. Yarborough of Texas also went to the hospital; he was the first to speak to the press.

Photograph: Sen. Yarborough at Parkland Hospital. He appears to be weeping.

McGEE and RYAN comment on Secret Service protection on a Presidential parade route.

McGEE: It is virtually impossible to check every route window in every building.

RYAN: West German Chancellor Erhard has expressed the deep grief of the German people. In Rome, Cardinal McIntyre and others were called together to recite prayers. Georges Pompidou of France called the act "atrocious."

3:27 pm
WASHINGTON, D.C.

BRINKLEY: Sen. Edward Kennedy of Massachusetts and Eunice Kennedy Shriver arrived at the White House a few minutes ago to go to Andrews Air Force Base—perhaps to fly to Dallas. Robert Kennedy will fly to Texas. Congress has recessed, and several members of Congress have given their reaction to the President's death. Sen. Mike Mansfield of Montana is "shocked." Sen. Alan Bible of Nevada calls it "one of the great tragedies of our lifetime." Sen. Harry Byrd of Virginia is "deeply shocked." Similar sentiments are being expressed by all members of Congress.

3:30 pm
WHITE HOUSE

On Camera: A crowd of people standing in Lafayette Park across from the West Wing of the White House.

3:31 pm
WASHINGTON, D.C.

BRINKLEY: George Reedy, an assistant to Lyndon Johnson, has arrived at the White House. We do not know at this time whether Johnson has been sworn in as President.

3:32 pm
NEW YORK

McGEE: We have no further report on the assassin. The search is continuing.

RYAN: Mrs. Kennedy and the body of the late President were escorted from the hospital by police. Mrs. Kennedy came out appearing somewhat dazed, and in shock. Ironically, most of the reporters did not know that President Kennedy was dead until they arrived at the hospital. Robert MacNeil, who was three cars behind the President, reports that newsmen didn't even know about the shooting.... The body of the late President will arrive at Andrews Air Force Base in Washington at 5:30 pm.

IRVING R. LEVINE (voice over from Rome): The President of Italy has called the death of President Kennedy "a great loss to humanity."

MacNEIL (on phone from Dallas): We will have a picture in about 15 minutes.... Dr. Malcolm Perry reported that the President arrived at Parkland Hospital in critical condition with neck and head injuries. Dr.

Friday, Nov. 22, 1963

William Kemp Clark, chief of neurosurgery, said the President was near death on arrival. A tracheotomy was performed, and the President was given blood transfusions, oxygen and, after his heart failed, external massage. The President died at 1:00 pm Dallas time—about twenty minutes after arrival at Parkland Hospital. He was wounded in the back of the head and on the right side of the head; there was a loss of blood and brain tissue. A bullet struck him in front as he faced the assailant. He never regained consciousness.... Lyndon Johnson is remaining in Dallas.

Dr. Malcolm Perry

3:40 pm
DALLAS
RYAN: A suspect has been taken into custody.

Film: Merchandise Mart in Dallas, where President Kennedy was to address a group of the city's leading citizens. At the time the films were taken, the President had been shot, but his condition was still unknown. An unidentified man at the rostrum offers a prayer for President Kennedy.

3:43 pm
NEW YORK
RYAN: A man has been arrested for the shooting of a Dallas policeman. There has been no arrest yet for the murder of President Kennedy.

3:48 pm
WASHINGTON, D.C.
BRINKLEY: The body of the late President will arrive at Andrews Air Force Base at 5:30 pm. Church bells are sounding in Washington. People are crying freely. NBC Newsman Robert Abernethy has reported that Sen. Edward Kennedy and Eunice Shriver have left Otis Air Force Base for Massachusetts.... Military officers in charge of state funerals are already in action. We assume that the Army will be in charge of details.

3:50 pm
WHITE HOUSE
RICHARD VALERIANI: The White House flag is flying at half-staff. The President's children, Caroline and John-John, are at the White House, as are Kennedy assistants McGeorge Bundy and Theodore Sorensen.

The air of grimness is reflected in the trees, which are bare of leaves.

On Camera: The crowd gathering on the sidewalk closest to the White House, behind the picket fence. Policemen are moving the crowd along.

VALERIANI: George Reedy is already at the White House. The White House press office mood is "stunned." Most news now is originating from Dallas.

3:53 pm
WASHINGTON, D.C.

AGRONSKY reads a statement by Sen. Barry Goldwater (R-Ariz.): "It is both shocking and dreadful that a thing like this could happen in a free country. The President's death is a profound loss to the nation and the free world. He and I were personal friends. It is also a great loss to me. Mrs. Goldwater and I offer our heartfelt sympathies to Mrs. Kennedy and the President's family." Agronsky adds that Sen. Goldwater has canceled all political appearances for the time being. Agronsky goes on to recall the 1960 Presidential campaign—in particular, a discussion he had with Gov. Connally about the likelihood of Lyndon Johnson's accepting the Vice-Presidential spot on the Kennedy ticket. Connally, a close friend of Lyndon Johnson, felt he would not accept. Agronsky disagreed. They wagered $50— a bet which, of course, Agronsky won.

3:56 pm
NEW YORK

RYAN: A report from Dallas has just come in: President Lyndon Baines Johnson has taken the oath of office on the Presidential plane. He was sworn in at 2:38 pm Central time. District Judge Sarah T. Hughes administered the oath of office to the 36th President. She is the first woman to perform this duty.... President Eisenhower has issued a statement: "I share the sense of shock and dismay that the entire nation must feel at the despicable act that took the life of the nation's President. On the personal side, Mrs. Eisenhower and I share the grief that Mrs. Kennedy must now feel, and we send to

her our prayerful thoughts and sympathetic sentiments in this hour."

3:58 pm McGEE: The Russians are broadcasting funeral music on the radio. Our Ambassador to Russia, Foy D. Kohler, has been informed of President Kennedy's death. Russian papers are saying that right-wing elements killed President Kennedy.... Lyndon Johnson is still in Dallas. Sen. Edward Kennedy and his sister, Eunice Shriver, are on their way to the family home in Hyannis Port from Otis Air Force Base. Mrs. Jacqueline Kennedy is with the new President and Mrs. Johnson.

RYAN summarizes the events from the start of the motorcade to the point at which President Kennedy was taken to Parkland Memorial Hospital.

Scenes at Houston, November 21

RYAN: By the time Kennedy had arrived, there was nothing medical science could do to save his life. There is no indication that the sniper has been found; however, one suspect has been taken in.

Film: The first unedited news film of today's Presidential motorcade. At 12:20 pm the motorcade is proceeding peacefully westward, when confusion suddenly sets in. Cars, trees and human figures tumble wildly before the camera. When the camera steadies, the motorcade is seen racing toward the hospital. The scene shifts to Parkland Hospital, where the camera shows the entrance to the emergency room.

On Camera: Outside the hospital. The camera focuses on a young boy in the crowd holding a placard reading, "Yankee, Go Home."

4:06 pm RYAN: Those were unedited, first-shown
NEW YORK scenes—that is a precious piece of film.

McGEE: Herbert Hoover has sent a message of condolence to Mrs. Kennedy and the Kennedy children.

RYAN: We are now going to show the last formal film of President John F. Kennedy,

taken last night in Houston, Texas. Along with Mrs. Kennedy, the President attended a testimonial dinner for Rep. Albert Thomas. His basic mission in Texas was to smooth a rift in the Democratic Party.

Film: Portions of President Kennedy's Houston speech last night.

RYAN: The Presidential plane is now airborne, carrying Lyndon Johnson to Washington. Present at the swearing-in of President Johnson were Mrs. Kennedy, Mrs. Johnson and several staffers. Judge Sarah Hughes wept while administering the oath.

4:14 pm
WASHINGTON, D.C.
ELIE ABEL: The guess here is that President Johnson will continue the foreign policy set up by President Kennedy.

4:15 pm
NEW YORK
RYAN: More news from Dallas concerning the assassin. . . . A rifle was found on the fifth floor of the Book Depository. . . . The police received a tip that the man who shot and killed the policeman entered a movie theatre. . . . The man has been captured.

4:16 pm
DALLAS
Tape Repeat: Brend's eyewitness account of the shooting.

MURPHY interviews eyewitnesses Mary Norman and Jean Hill, who photographed the President and Mrs. Kennedy slumped over in the car. (The Polaroid snap shot appears on camera.) They describe hearing the shots ring out and Mrs. Kennedy crying, "My God, he's been shot."

4:23 pm
MURPHY: There is little doubt that 24-year-old Lee Oswald, the suspect picked up earlier, is the slayer of the Dallas policeman. Eyewitnesses report that Oswald brandished a pistol and shouted, "It's all over now." Oswald worked as a stock man at the Depository, and is reported to be a defector. He is the same man picked up earlier in the theater.

4:26 pm
DALLAS
MURPHY: Lee Harvey Oswald, the man picked up in the theater, applied for Russian citizenship on Nov. 1, 1959. He is married to a Russian woman. Dallas police say the

24-year-old Oswald shot and killed Officer J. D. Tippit and might be connected with the assassination of President Kennedy.

4:28 pm
NEW YORK

RYAN: Gov. Connally's condition is very serious. It is not critical.

McGEE: Lyndon Johnson should be in Washington within an hour and a half.

RYAN: There is little else to report now. President and Mrs. Johnson and Mrs. Kennedy should be back in Washington by 6:05 this evening.

McGEE: News of President Kennedy's death is being withheld from his 98-year-old grandmother.

Film: President and Mrs. Kennedy arrive at the San Antonio, Texas, airport. (Portions of their arrival were telecast locally.) From the landing platform President Kennedy speaks about the space age.

4:34 pm
WASHINGTON, D.C.

PETER HACKES: People here are speechless. . . . John F. Kennedy, the first President of the new Space Age, wanted the future of outer space to be peaceful. Lyndon Johnson is expected to pound hard on the space program. . . . The Pentagon is in a state of shock. . . . A number of people are at the White House now to discuss the funeral.

4:39 pm
NEW YORK

RYAN reads the statement issued by U.N. Ambassador Adlai Stevenson: "The tragedy of this day is beyond instant comprehension. All of us who knew him will bear the grief of his death to the day of ours. And all the men everywhere who love peace and justice and freedom will bow their heads. At such a moment we can only turn to prayer—prayer to comfort our grief, to sustain Mrs. Kennedy and his family, to strengthen President Johnson and to guide us in time to come. May God help us."

McGEE: It is now apparent that no Secret Service man was injured. A Dallas policeman was killed. . . . It is reported that Mrs. Kennedy turned to the President just before the

Lee Harvey Oswald:
As a marine, in U.S.S.R. with Marina, portrait in Russia, two pictures from period as pro-Cuba agitator

shooting and said, "You can't say Dallas wasn't kind to us." She cradled her husband all the way to the hospital. Mrs. Kennedy appears to be stunned. Her first thoughts are to be with her children.

4:42 pm
DALLAS

Film: Outside Parkland Hospital, Mrs. Kennedy is seen conferring with the Dallas police. The camera shows the Presidential car, roses lying on the back seat. A Secret Service man is seen pounding his fist on the car.

4:49 pm
WASHINGTON, D.C.

AGRONSKY: Lyndon Johnson assumes the Presidential office with a vast amount of government experience. He is a man who has accomplished much in office. While Kennedy was President, Johnson gained considerable insight into the office he now assumes.

4:54 pm
NEW YORK

RYAN: Lee Oswald seems to be the prime suspect in the assassination of John F. Kennedy.

On Camera: Scenes of the Texas School Book Depository, from where the shots were fired, and the rifle being removed from the building.

McGEE: Oswald is still only a suspect.... The President's body will lie in state until Monday. The actual funeral service will probably be held in Boston.

Photograph: President John F. Kennedy.

GOV. NELSON ROCKEFELLER (R-NY; voice over): The assassination of the President is a shocking and terrible tragedy for the nation, and the world. John F. Kennedy was the youngest President in the history of our nation. He brought to this high office years of experience in the House of Representatives and the Senate of the United States. And during the Second World War he distinguished himself by an outstanding record of military service. His was a life of service to the nation, of concern for his fellow man, of faith in God and belief in human freedom. The people of the State of New York, together with all other American peoples throughout the world, mourn the untimely death of John Fitzgerald Kennedy, 35th President of the United States.

Now, therefore, I, Nelson A. Rockefeller, Governor of the State of New York, do hereby direct that all flags on public buildings in the state be flown at half-staff for the 30 days next ensuing, and I designate that period as one of public mourning for the deceased President of the United States, and I do further direct that all state offices be closed on the day of the funeral services.

5:01 pm
THREE NETWORK POOL, NEW YORK

GEN. DWIGHT EISENHOWER: We all share a sense of shock and dismay over this despicable act.... I was at a UN meeting when the announcement came.... Americans are a loyal people; however, there is bound to be a psychotic sort of accident sometime.

5:08 pm
WASHINGTON, D.C.

VALERIANI: The Kennedy children have not been told of their father's death yet. Special Secret Service agents have been assigned to protect Speaker of the House John McCormack, the next man in Presidential succession after Lyndon Johnson.

5:10 pm
NEW YORK

McGEE: Prayers were offered in New Ross, Ireland, home of President Kennedy's ancestors.

SEN. J. W. FULBRIGHT (D-Ark.; audio only): This is a tragedy beyond words—an unspeakable crime. The Kennedy family has lost a loved one; I have lost a friend. In the face of sudden tragedy, the nation will continue to function. The new President Johnson is a man of long experience. We must all unite behind our new President.

5:13 pm
WASHINGTON, D.C.

AGRONSKY: The members of the Cabinet are all returning to Washington. President Johnson will select those he wants to retain in his administration.... The late President's body will lie in state in the Rotunda of the Capitol building. The burial will be either in Boston or in Arlington Cemetery—the

Arrow: Approximate location of President's car

Where shots were fired

Friday, Nov. 22, 1963

Kennedy family has not yet made this decision. The President's brother-in-law, Sargent Shriver, is in charge of funeral preparations.... The Cabinet is expected to rally around the new President. Lyndon Johnson was included in all meetings of the Cabinet under President Kennedy, as well as in all meetings of the National Security Council. It is too soon to speculate about Cabinet changes.... President Johnson will arrive in Washington about 15 minutes from now. As yet, he has made no statement.

5:18 pm
NEW YORK

McGEE: After taking the oath as our 36th President, Lyndon Johnson was quoted as saying, "Let's get this plane back to Washington."

5:19 pm
BONN,
GERMANY

WELLES HANGEN (audio only): Because of the fear of possible invasion, an alert condition— the highest emergency short of war—has been proclaimed in West Germany.... Chancellor Erhard was due to visit to meet with President Kennedy. Former Chancellor Konrad Adenauer, who had criticized Kennedy's policy, said today that the President gave his life for peace.... The entire Western world has been caught off balance.

5:23 pm
LONDON

KENNETH BERNSTEIN (audio only): Queen Elizabeth has been informed of the assassination.... A crowd is gathering outside the American Embassy in London.

5:26 pm
WHITE HOUSE

RAY SCHERER describes the plan for President Johnson's arrival, and the funeral arrangements for the late President Kennedy.

5:27 pm
NEW YORK

McGEE: Four out of five of our major allies have seen a change in their government in 1963.... The plane carrying President Johnson and the body of the late President Kennedy is on its way to Washington right now.

5:29 pm
WEST BERLIN

JOHN CHANCELLOR (audio only): People are walking through the streets asking if it is true.... Mayor Willy Brandt of West Berlin has asked the people to light candles in their

30

windows tonight. Students will march in memory of President Kennedy.

5:32 pm
NEW YORK

McGEE: It is reported that Gov. John B. Connally is in good condition, and will recover from his wounds.

RYAN: At no time has Mrs. Jacqueline Kennedy lost her composure, although her clothes were spattered with President Kennedy's blood.

5:36 pm

Photograph: Lee Harvey Oswald, the prime suspect in the murder of President Kennedy. **Photograph:** Lyndon Johnson taking the oath of office as 36th President of the United States.

RYAN: At 10:00 am tomorrow, President Kennedy's family will view the casket, followed by Supreme Court Justices, Governors, Senators and members of the Diplomatic Corps. The public will be permitted to view the body later. Plans for the funeral service have not been set.

5:42 pm
ROME

LEVINE (audio only): Pope Paul VI stated that he is profoundly stricken by this shocking crime, and deplores this event with all his heart. He expresses the hope that it will not damage the American people. On meeting the first Catholic President of the United States he found him a man of great wisdom. . . . The Pope will offer a holy mass for his soul.

5:44 pm
NEW YORK

McGEE comments on President Kennedy's speech during the Cuban crisis.

RYAN quotes from the prepared speech President Kennedy was to have given in Dallas today: "We are watchmen on the walls of world freedom to achieve the ancient vision of peace on earth. . . .'Except the Lord keep the city, the watchman waketh but in vain.'"

McGEE reads Sir Winston Churchill's statement on the assassination: "This monstrous act has taken from us a great statesman and a wise and valiant man. . . . Those who come after Mr. Kennedy must

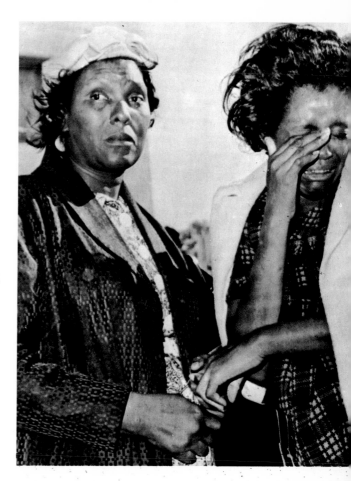

31

Friday, Nov. 22, 1963

strive the more to achieve the ideals of world peace and human happiness to which his Presidency was dedicated." McGee then reads the reaction of Gov. Richard Hughes of New Jersey: "In the battle for freedom, President Kennedy never flinched.... To President Johnson should go our prayers and the dedication of every one of us."

RYAN: Suspected assassin Lee Harvey Oswald was a member of a pro-Castro committee in New Orleans, and had renounced his U.S. citizenship. In a gunfight with two Dallas policemen, he shot and killed one of them, saying, "It's all over now." Oswald was an employee of the building where the sniper's nest was discovered—a building not far from where the motorcade passed.

McGEE: The Kennedys were enjoying their trip to Texas.... Mrs. Kennedy has conducted herself in irreproachable fashion since the shooting. She helped take her husband to the hospital.... Blood-stained roses were left on the back seat of the car.... Mrs. Kennedy was present at the swearing-in of the new President.

RYAN: There was never the least hope of saving the President's life. The priest said that when he arrived to administer last rites, the President was already dead. He drew back the sheet and saw him.

6:04 pm
ANDREWS AIR FORCE BASE, WASHINGTON, D.C.
ROBERT ABERNETHY: Several thousand people are here at Andrews Air Force Base awaiting the arrival of Lyndon B. Johnson and the body of President Kennedy.

On Camera: The Presidential jet is seen arriving, along with an Army helicopter. The huge plane lands, and the casket containing the late President's body is lifted out. Nancy Dickerson comments along with Abernethy as the casket is lowered from the plane by means of a special elevator; lifted from the elevator by a waiting Honor Guard; and placed in a Navy ambulance for

transportation to Bethesda Naval Hospital. Attorney General Robert F. Kennedy escorts Mrs. Jacqueline Kennedy to the ambulance. She gets in, and the ambulance drives away. ... Lyndon Johnson, Mrs. Johnson and several aides cross the airfield to a bank of microphones. Lyndon Johnson makes his first public statement as President of the United States.

PRESIDENT JOHNSON: This is a sad time for all people. We have suffered a loss that cannot be weighed. For me it is a deep personal tragedy. I know the world shares the sorrow that Mrs. Kennedy and her family bear. I will do my best. That is all I can do. I ask for your help—and God's.

On Camera: A group of Senators gather around President Johnson. Mrs. Mansfield, wife of Sen. Mike Mansfield, is shown weeping. President Johnson moves toward the helicopter to speak to McGeorge Bundy and other advisers to the late President.

NANCY DICKERSON: Sen. George Aiken of Vermont said that he is just beginning to realize what has happened. ... Telephone circuits have been hastily organized. ... The helicopter is about to take Lyndon Johnson to the White House. Inside the helicopter, President Johnson is still talking with aides to the late President Kennedy.

On Camera: The helicopter takes off, leaving Andrews Air Force Base. The Honor Guard departs. The late President's baggage is taken off the Presidential jet.

6:21 pm
NEW YORK **RYAN:** President Kennedy's body will go to Bethesda Naval Hospital to be prepared for burial. Tomorrow it will lie in state in the East Room of the White House. Members of Congress will go to pay their respects. President Johnson will meet with leaders of both parties.

McGEE quotes statement by former Vice President Richard Nixon: "The assassination of the President is a terrible tragedy for the

nation. Mrs. Nixon and I have sent a personal message expressing our deepest sympathy to the members of the family in this hour of sorrow."

RYAN: Navy ships will fire a salute in honor of the late President. It is ironic that John Kennedy went through World War II and then lost his life in this unbelievable fashion. . . . President Johnson is on his way to the White House.

6:26 pm
WHITE HOUSE
ROBERT GORALSKI (voice over): The helicopter carrying President and Mrs. Johnson has just landed.

On Camera: President and Mrs. Johnson walk across the lawn to the White House. Secretary of Defense Robert McNamara talks with the President as they walk.

6:29 pm
NEW YORK
McGEE: The man who was arrested—Lee Oswald—is being interrogated. . . . Expressions of regret are coming in from all parts of the world.

STATION IDENTIFICATION

6:32 pm
WASHINGTON, D.C.
BRINKLEY: President Kennedy was shot at 1:00 p.m. today and died one half hour later. President Lyndon Johnson took the oath of office in the Presidential jet and is now at the White House in Washington, D.C.

6:47 pm
WHITE HOUSE
GORALSKI: Presidential advisers Sorensen and Bundy heard the reports on television and radio. . . . There was a feeling of disbelief, followed by mournful recognition when the flags were lowered. . . . The Kennedy children still have not been told that their father is dead.

6:49 pm
WASHINGTON, D.C.
BRINKLEY: A mass for the late President will be offered by Richard Cardinal Cushing of Boston, long-time friend of the Kennedy family.

6:55 pm
CHICAGO
Film: Mourners praying in a Chicago church. NBC Newsman Floyd Kalber describes the scene.

Friday, Nov. 22, 1963

On Camera: A series of views of Washington, D.C. Flags flying at half-staff; the Russian Embassy; people standing dazed in Lafayette Park across Pennsylvania Avenue from the White House. Brinkley introduces a sequence of filmed statements by prominent men in Washington.

SEN. JENNINGS RANDOLPH (D-W. Va.): I would like to express profound sadness at his going. . . .

SEN. MIKE MANSFIELD: Kennedy was a good, decent man with so much on his shoulders. . . .

SEN. EVERETT McKINLEY DIRKSEN: This act is incredible. . . . It leaves one speechless.

SEN. RICHARD B. RUSSELL: President Kennedy was a dedicated statesman.

SEN. HUGH SCOTT: We must all rally to the support of President Johnson.

7:00 pm
NEW YORK **HUNTLEY:** The Dallas police are holding suspect Lee Oswald. In 1959, Oswald wanted to become a Russian citizen. He said getting out of the U.S. was like getting out of prison.

Tape (audio only): Interview with Lee Oswald in New Orleans held August 21, 1963, at station WDSU-TV.

HUNTLEY: Oswald had become involved with the police because of his activities with the "Fair Play for Cuba Committee." He called himself a Marxist.

Tape: President Kennedy's Inaugural Address—the full text, as seen and heard on January 20, 1961.

Tape: President Kennedy's Cuban Crisis speech, Oct. 22, 1962.

HUNTLEY: That may have been the supreme hour of courage in President Kennedy's life.

Tape: President Kennedy's speech on civil rights, June 11, 1963.

HUNTLEY comments on the Kennedy administration's achievements in outer space.

Cuba Crisis: With Gen. David Shoup and Adm. George Anderson

With Astronaut John Glenn and Vice President Johnson

7:43 pm
LOS ANGELES

ROY NEAL: In the first year of the Kennedy administration, the space program underwent a realignment. Lyndon Johnson, then Vice President, became Chairman of the National Aeronautics and Space Council. President Kennedy enjoyed friendships with John Glenn and the other astronauts. He believed much could be done through co-operation with the Soviet Union in space research.

Tape Repeat: Interview with Lee Oswald, station WDSU-TV, New Orleans, this time with sound as well as video.

REPORTER: Are you a Marxist?

OSWALD: Well, I have studied Marxist philosophy, yes sir.

REPORTER: But are you a Marxist? I think you did admit on an earlier radio interview that you consider yourself a Marxist.

OSWALD: Well, I would definitely say that I am a Marxist; that is correct. But that does not mean, however, that I'm a communist. [Oswald goes on to explain what he feels are the differences between Marxism and Russian communism, and outlines the aims of the "Fair Play for Cuba Committee."]

Film: President Kennedy speaks in Fort Worth, Texas. He describes his wife, Jacqueline, explaining that while she takes longer getting dressed than he does, she always looks better. Mrs. Kennedy enters and joins the late President. Vice President Lyndon Johnson also appears on this film.

8:01 pm
WASHINGTON, D.C.

BRINKLEY: President Johnson has called a meeting at the White House tonight with leaders of the Congress.

WHITE HOUSE

SCHERER interviews Charles Roberts, correspondent for Newsweek, who was present at the swearing-in of President Johnson. He describes how Mrs. Kennedy, still in blood-stained clothes, stood next to Lyndon Johnson as he took the oath of office.

Friday, Nov. 22, 1963

8:05 pm
WASHINGTON, D.C.
BRINKLEY: The burial will take place in Arlington National Cemetery or in Brookline, Mass. The President's body will lie in state at the White House tomorrow. At noon on Sunday his body will lie in state in the Capitol Rotunda. . . . The late President was a man of youth and vigor—a man who enjoyed being President. Lyndon Johnson is expected to carry on the Kennedy tradition.

8:17 pm
DALLAS
MURPHY: Suspect Lee Oswald has been taken to a secret location.

8:19 pm
NEW YORK
RYAN: Every candle is lit at St. Patrick's Cathedral. Saks Fifth Avenue has curtains drawn across all its display windows.

8:20 pm
TIMES SQUARE, NEW YORK
GABE PRESSMAN: A patrolman told me he has never seen Times Square like this. Theaters are shut down; there is an overwhelming feeling of sadness among the people.

8:23 pm
WHITE HOUSE
SCHERER: Acting Press Secretary Andrew Hatcher reported at a news conference that President Johnson met with leaders of Congress for 45 minutes and asked for their support in this time of tragedy. The Congressional leaders assured President Johnson of their bipartisan support. . . . Mrs. Kennedy has left the White House.

8:25 pm
NEW YORK
McGEE: The prime suspect, Lee Oswald, is being held in Dallas, still claiming he did not do it. Police describe him as a calculating man—very arrogant. He has been charged with the killing of the policeman.

McGEE: The Naval ambulance has taken the body of the President to Bethesda Naval Hospital for burial preparation. The body will be taken to the White House early tomorrow morning.

8:34 pm
RADIO CITY MUSIC HALL, NEW YORK
GEOFFREY POND conducts on-the-street interviews. An Indian visitor says, "We have lost a friend."

Film: Highlights of John F. Kennedy's life and career. Inauguration Day, Jan. 20, 1961.

a. Birthplace in Brookline
b. Early portraits: JFK at left
c. At right
d. On kiddie car
e. Football at Dexter Academy

38

c   a   b

d

e

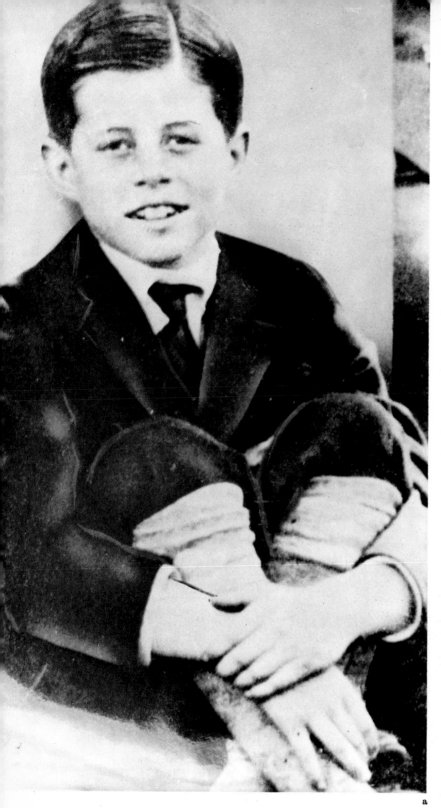

a

b

d

e

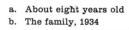

a. About eight years old
b. The family, 1934
c. Harvard freshman football squad, 1936
d. With Princeton roommates, 1935
e. At Harvard, 1936
f. With mother, 1938
g. In 1941
h. Bound for England with father, 1939

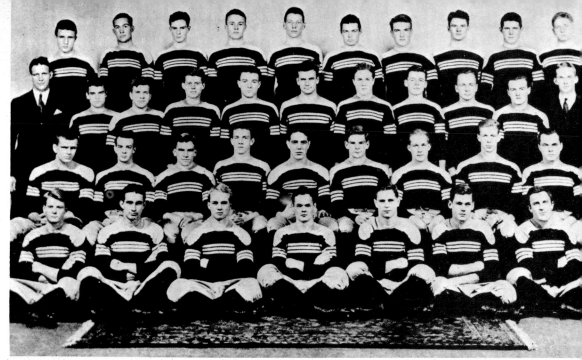

c

h

f

g

a

b

c

d

a. Ensign Kennedy with inductees, 1942
b. With PT 109 crew, 1943
c. Lieutenant (jg), 1943
d. Lieutenant, 1944
e. With FDR, Jr., and Robert F. Wagner, 1948
f. As Massachusetts Congressman, 1945
g. Jacqueline Bouvier, Hyannis Port, 1953
h. Entering hospital, 1954
i. Senator, on Capitol steps

e

f

g

h

i

Friday, Nov. 22, 1963

8:50 pm
NEW YORK

McGEE: It has been established that Oswald was in the building where the shot that killed the President was fired.

9:02 pm
NEW YORK

McGEE: Lee Oswald still insists he had nothing to do with the killing. He was picked up four miles from the Depository. Dallas policeman J. D. Tippit was shot and killed while pursuing Oswald. Both Oswald and his brother were questioned by the F.B.I. Oswald's wife is Russian and does not speak English. . . . The woman cashier at the theater says Oswald came in shortly after she had heard of the assassination. The police raced into the theater. The house lights were turned on. Oswald stood up and said, "This is it."

9:05 pm
WASHINGTON,
D.C.

BRINKLEY: Mrs. Jacqueline Kennedy has gone into seclusion with her children.

9:12 pm
WHITE HOUSE

McGEE: Mrs. Jacqueline Kennedy sat beside the casket of her husband on the plane from Dallas to Washington.

NEW YORK

McGEE: President Lyndon Johnson phoned Mrs. Joseph Kennedy, the late President's mother, from the Presidential plane. He then placed a call to Mrs. John Connally, wife of the wounded Governor of Texas.

9:25 pm
WHITE HOUSE

SCHERER: Secretary of State Dean Rusk is on his way back to see the new President. President Eisenhower will meet with President Johnson tomorrow. . . . Doctors in charge of Gov. John Connally are in touch with the White House, and the reports say that Connally is recovering.

9:27 pm
WASHINGTON,
D.C.

MUELLER: The stock market closed at word of the assassination. . . . The country President Kennedy left is in sound economic condition. Manufacturing is up, personal income and employment are up. And though unemployment is now at five million, this is in a country facing increased automation. . . . This nation has never been richer or stronger.

J. D. Tippit

44

AGRONSKY: After the initial shock, President Kennedy's secretary began methodically removing the mementos from his desk— the family pictures, the PT109 souvenir— making ready for the new President's arrival. This swift preparation is a meaningful gesture, symbolic of the continuity of government.

BRINKLEY: One of the mementos on President Kennedy's desk was a silver calendar outlining the days of the Cuban crisis.

9:35 pm
NEW YORK
McGEE lists the Presidents who died or were assassinated while in office, observing that another Vice President who succeeded to the Presidency after an assassination was named Johnson.

9:39 pm
NEW YORK
RYAN: President Johnson telephoned Mrs. Joseph Kennedy, mother of the late President. He is reported to have said, "My God, I wish I knew how to tell you." President Johnson also put in a call to Mrs. John Connally in Dallas and spoke with her briefly.

9:48 pm
NEW YORK
McGEE reads excerpts from London newspapers. Mirror: We have lost our champion. John F. Kennedy was gentle and magnanimous in victory. He held firm against communism. Times: John F. Kennedy stood for many hopeful ideas of history. Daily Express: The Cuban crisis depicted John F. Kennedy's supreme courage. This event may have changed the course of history. The United States will require all the steadfastness, forebearance and courage it can muster. Daily Telegraph: President Kennedy's greatest contribution was the signing of the Test Ban Treaty. He helped the U.S. rise to its peak. Daily Sketch: John F. Kennedy was a man of courage. His finest hour was during the Cuban crisis. It was the ultimate test of human mettle.

RYAN: Lee Harvey Oswald was arrested earlier in New Orleans this summer for

handing out literature on the "Fair Play for Cuba Committee." Station WDSU-TV in New Orleans had Oswald on a program called "Conversation Carte Blanche," where he stated that he was a Marxist, that he had married in Russia, and that he was now a member of "Fair Play for Cuba." Oswald was in the building where the shots that killed President Kennedy were fired. He is now in custody and is still being questioned.

10:01 pm
WASHINGTON, D.C.

BRINKLEY: Lyndon Johnson is on his way to "The Elms," his home in northwest Washington.

EDWIN NEWMAN: This event is unreal, absurd—one of the things we just don't let happen. But if one in one hundred ninety million wants to kill the President, he will. The unpleasant truth about America is that it is a country of violence. Violence plays a part in our very lives—yet what we worry about is our image abroad. Today, America does not appear to be an adult country. Emotions run high—regional, religious and economic. We must begin at the top, for the political climate is set by the President. In the days to come we will hear much of how we must stick together. It is within our power to take our public life more seriously than we have. Americans tonight are a grossly diminished people.

BRINKLEY: If we have come to the point where a President cannot appear in public without fear of being shot, then we are less civilized than we think we are.

10:08 pm
BOSTON
(WBZ-TV)

ARCH McDONALD interviews Richard Cardinal Cushing prior to his departure for Hyannis Port.

CARDINAL CUSHING: John Kennedy was a ◄ devoted friend, dedicated to God and country. In his Inaugural Address he said, "I shall not shrink from my responsibilities." He has filled that pledge with his life. May the good Lord inspire us to know and learn the total dedication and loyalty that John

Kennedy displayed and, in his youthful
vigor, bestowed to us. May God rest
his noble soul.

10:11 pm **McGEE** comments on how Secret Service men
NEW YORK respond to any crisis while protecting the
President, recalling an incident that occurred
on one of President Eisenhower's trips.
RYAN recalls how Secret Service agents
held back a woman as she rushed up to shake
hands with President Kennedy.
Film and Tape: The President's day,
Thursday, Nov. 21. In the morning, the
President and Mrs. Kennedy board the
Presidential plane in Washington for Texas.
They arrive in San Antonio, and with Gov.
and Mrs. John Connally, ride in an open
motorcade through the city. At the luncheon
which follows, President Kennedy delivers
a speech dedicating the six million dollar
Aerospace Medical Health Center at Brooks
Air Force Base. . . . Dallas Police Chief

Jesse Curry is shown outlining the
precautions taken for the President's trip
to Dallas. Curry states that he doesn't
anticipate any trouble of the sort that greeted
Adlai Stevenson on his visit to Dallas.
Preparations have been made for controlling
unruly crowds; certain individuals have
been placed under special surveillance. . . .
President and Mrs. Kennedy arrive in
Houston; the President goes into the crowd to
shake some hands. The motorcade takes
them to the testimonial dinner honoring
Rep. Albert Thomas, who has been
instrumental in bringing the giant new space
center to Houston. Lyndon Johnson speaks
first, recalling the late Sam Rayburn's reply
when asked about the influence of Texas
on national affairs: "In Texas we pick them
honest, we pick them young, we send them
to Washington and we keep them there."
President Kennedy then touches off a storm
of laughter by congratulating Rep. Thomas

Friday, Nov. 22, 1963

for having a part in "firing the largest payroll into space. Er, payload. [Laughter.] Well, it will also be our largest payroll." He goes on to speak of the space age: "In 1990, your children will be applying what we are learning today about space travel. . . . In 1990, the Age of Space will be entering its second stage, and America will be first in space."

STATION IDENTIFICATION

RYAN: Oswald was given $437 by the American government for the return trip home from Moscow.

10:29 pm
WHITE HOUSE

SANDER VANOCUR: President Johnson left about an hour ago for his home in Washington. Before leaving, he conferred with Defense Secretary McNamara, Under Secretary of State George Ball and FBI Chief J. Edgar Hoover. Johnson will arrive at the White House in the morning and meet with Secretary of State Dean Rusk. He is scheduled to meet with former President Eisenhower at 11:30 am. . . . Mrs. Jacqueline Kennedy is at Bethesda, Md. She is remaining near the body of the late President. The President's body will lie in state in the East Room tomorrow. Sunday it will be moved to the Rotunda of the Capitol Building where the public will be permitted to view the casket. The Kennedy children have been taken from the White House to an undisclosed location. It is not known whether they have been told the tragic news.

10:32 pm
WASHINGTON, D.C.

ABERNETHY: Capitol leaders are planning on carrying on their work until December.

10:35 pm
DALLAS

MURPHY interviews Sarah T. Hughes, the judge who administered the oath of office to Lyndon Johnson. She explains that she received a call requesting her to officiate at the swearing-in. She found a Bible and the oath of office waiting on the plane. There were about 25 people present, including Mrs. Johnson, Mrs. Kennedy and several

Judge Sarah T. Hughes

48

Congressmen. Mrs. Kennedy had sent word that she wished to be present, and she stood beside President Johnson during the ceremony. After the President had taken the oath of office, he immediately ordered the plane to Washington.

10:38 pm
NEW YORK

HUNTLEY reads the complete text of President Kennedy's speech scheduled to be given at the annual meeting of the Dallas Citizens Council: "[The] link between leadership and learning is not only essential at the community level. It is even more indispensable in world affairs.... Today other voices are heard in the land— voices preaching doctrines wholly unrelated to reality, wholly unsuited to the sixties, doctrines which apparently assume that words will suffice without weapons, that vituperation is as good as victory, and that peace is a sign of weakness.... We in this country, in this generation, are—by destiny rather than choice—the watchmen on the walls of world freedom. We ask, therefore, that we may be worthy of our power and responsibility—that we may exercise our strength with wisdom and restraint—and that we may achieve in our time and for all time the ancient vision of peace on earth, goodwill toward men. That must always be our goal— and the righteousness of our cause must always underlie our strength. For as was written long ago: 'Except the Lord keep the city, the watchman waketh but in vain.' "

10:59 pm
WASHINGTON, D.C.

DICKERSON: President Johnson has arrived at his home. As he drove up, he acknowledged the greetings of the people waiting for him. The wrought-iron gates are closed, the activity subdued. The Secret Service men who accompanied President Johnson carried their guns in the open. Mrs. Johnson said that the whole event is like a nightmare.

11:03 pm
HOUSTON (KPRC-TV)

Tape: Ray Muller interviews Lyndon Johnson ◄ on his ranch. (This interview, taped Sept. 27, 1963, was to be shown locally.) Johnson

tells how his family first came to Texas. He explains that his father and mother were both interested in public life, and that he himself has always been deeply interested in politics. He states he is proud to be an American, and feels that ours is the greatest form of government on earth.

11:18 pm
DALLAS

Film: Mayor Earle Cabell of Dallas.

MAYOR CABELL: The city of Dallas is in shock. . . . I have never seen so many people turn out for an event as came to see the motorcade this afternoon. The people of Dallas displayed such warmth. . . . And then, after 12 or 13 miles, to have those shots ring out. . . . It is hard to believe. . . . But I don't believe this event will hurt Dallas as a city. This was the act of a maniac who could have lived anywhere—a man who belonged to no city.

11:21 pm
NEW YORK

MURPHY: The churches of Dallas are open.

11:21 pm
NEW YORK

RYAN reads Gen. Douglas MacArthur's letter to Mrs. Jacqueline Kennedy: "I realize the utter futility of words at such a time, but the world of civilization shares the poignancy of this monumental tragedy. As a former comrade in arms, his death kills something within me."

MOBILE UNIT, ROCKEFELLER CENTER, NEW YORK

POND conducts on-the-street interviews. One man remembers President Kennedy as so full of dynamic energy that it is difficult to imagine him gone. A second is too shocked to say anything. A third man says he will always remember the Cuban crisis of Oct. 1962; he would have been proud to serve in the Armed Forces for John F. Kennedy. A fourth expresses the hope that President Johnson will carry on the late President's policies.

11:24 pm
NEW YORK

HUNTLEY quotes Rep. Henry B. Gonzales (D-Tex.) as having seen Mrs. Kennedy, in a last tribute to her husband, kiss his blood-stained lips and place her ring in his hand. "I just couldn't take it," Gonzales said. "It was just too much, emotionally."

Film: Statement by Sen. Hubert H. Humphrey (D-Minn.): "What irony that this should happen in the U.S., the land of freedom and dignity, which now somehow, has taken the life of our great and beloved leader. . . ."

Film: Statement by Sen. Everett McKinley Dirksen (R-Ill.): "Only someone suffering from aberrations of personality and motivated by insane passions would be guilty of the assassination of the great leader of the greatest country on earth. . . ."

BRINKLEY: Mrs. Kennedy and her two children will remain overnight at Bethesda Hospital.

11:37 pm
NEW YORK **Film:** Statement by Gov. Endicott Peabody (D-Mass.).

GOV. PEABODY: I am deeply grieved by the shocking, untimely and unbelievable death of our beloved President Kennedy at the hands of an assassin. He will live forever in the hearts and memories of people in our Massachusetts—his home state—our nation and throughout the world as a humanitarian and as a leader who gave his life for his principles and beliefs.

Film: A police officer emerges from the Book ◄ Depository with the murder weapon.

Photograph: President Kennedy slumped forward after the shooting.

Film Repeat: Outside Parkland Hospital.

Tape Repeat: Charles Brend's eyewitness account.

Photograph: The swearing-in of Lyndon Johnson as President.

Photograph: The Fort Worth movie theater where Lee Oswald was arrested for the murder of Dallas patrolman Tippit.

Film: Dallas City Jail.

TOM PETTIT (voice over): This is where Lee Oswald is being held. We can see Capt. Will Fritz, head of the Homicide Bureau, in the background. . . . Oswald is still being questioned.

Oswald under arrest

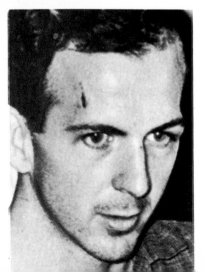

MacNEIL: The nation is still in shock from this tragic event. The city of Dallas wishes it had not happened here. . . .

11:57 pm
NEW YORK

McGEE: Oswald has been given paraffin tests to determine whether he had shot a rifle.

STATION IDENTIFICATION

McGEE: The Kennedy family wishes to ask that no flowers be sent, but that the money be used instead for donations to charity.

Prince and Princess Radziwill

11:58 pm
WHITE HOUSE

On Camera: The crowds assembled in Lafayette Square.

VALERIANI: The general reaction has been one of shock and disbelief.

12 midnight
NEW YORK

McGEE: Mrs. Jacqueline Kennedy is at Bethesda Naval Medical Center and is remaining near the body of the late President. She is not under sedation.

12:02 am
WASHINGTON, D.C.

NEWMAN: The death of President Kennedy has left French President Charles deGaulle the most experienced leader of the Western world in foreign affairs. This, however, does not mean he will be the leader. The U.S. remains dominant, but as Lyndon Johnson lacks the stature that John Kennedy held as a world leader, this situation may change. Our allies will most likely follow their own line of policy. Only if President Johnson wins the 1964 election will he have prestige with our allies. America's reaction to today's brutality will influence the way in which our allies—and Khrushchev—look upon our stability as a nation.

12:06 am

Tape: The requiem mass for President John Fitzgerald Kennedy held earlier Friday at St. John's Evangelist Catholic Church, Philadelphia, Pa. The celebrant is the Rev. Anthony J. O'Neill. Father John Lynch comments off-camera.

12:38 am

McGEE: Princess Lee Radziwill, younger sister of Mrs. Jacqueline Kennedy, will leave London tomorrow for the United States to be with her sister. . . . Sixty thousand Berliners gathered at Berlin City Hall to express ◄

Friday, Nov. 22, 1963

their grief at the death of President Kennedy. Chancellor Ludwig Erhard has announced he will attend the funeral if invited.

Salinger, Freeman, Dillon, Rusk, Udall, Hodges, Walter Heller, Wirtz

12:40 am

ANDREWS AIR FORCE, WASHINGTON, D.C.

On Camera: The arrival of the Cabinet.

HERB KAPLOW: En route to Japan when they received word of the assassination, the members of the Cabinet ordered their plane back to Washington. Secretary of State Dean Rusk is first off the plane, followed by Secretary of Commerce Luther Hodges; Secretary of the Interior Stewart Udall; Secretary of Agriculture Orville Freeman; Secretary of the Treasury Douglas Dillon; Secretary of Labor Willard Wirtz; and Presidential Press Secretary Pierre Salinger. They are being met at the plane by Protocol chief Angier Biddle Duke and Assistant Secretary of the Navy Franklin D. Roosevelt, Jr. The party is moving to the microphones. Dean Rusk will speak for the Cabinet.

DEAN RUSK: We have fully shared the deep sense of shock at the grievous loss the nation has suffered. Those of us who have had the honor of serving President Kennedy value the gallantry and wisdom he brought to the grave, awesome and lonely office of the Presidency. President Johnson needs and deserves our fullest support.

12:44 am

NEW YORK

McGEE comments on the incident that occurred last October in Dallas on "UN/US Day" during which right-wing elements picketed and spat upon Adlai Stevenson.

12:45 am

WASHINGTON, D.C.

AGRONSKY: Before the President went to Dallas, Adlai Stevenson called the White House and spoke with Arthur Schlesinger, Jr., recommending that President Kennedy reconsider his trip in light of that city's mood and attitude. Stevenson later called back and asked that his recommendation be withdrawn.

12:48 am

NEW YORK

McGEE: Mrs. Jacqueline Kennedy will return to the White House with the body of the late President when it is taken from Bethesda to the East Room.

HUNTLEY: The 1960 campaign and election were pure political drama. President Kennedy showed an appreciation for the great game of politics; reporters always enjoyed being around him. We will remember him always.

12:51 am
WASHINGTON, D.C.

BRINKLEY: We are about to wind up, as about all that could happen, has happened. It is one of the ugliest days in American history. There is seldom any time to think any more, and today there was none. In about four hours we had gone from President Kennedy in Dallas, alive, to back in Washington, dead, and a new President in his place. There is really no more to say except that what happened has been just too much, too ugly and too fast.

12:54 am
DALLAS

Tape: The empty auditorium in Austin, Texas, where President Kennedy was to have spoken; and the home of Lyndon Johnson, where President and Mrs. Kennedy were to have stayed as guests.

MacNEIL: One of the cooks at the LBJ ranch heard the news of the President's assassination on the radio, and informed the security agents already on the property, who, in turn, ordered the ranch placed under top security. . . . Oswald has been formally charged with the murder of President Kennedy.

Film: Oswald is heard to say, "I didn't shoot anybody." Lee Oswald protesting his innocence. Jerry Hill, Dallas police sergeant who apprehended Oswald in the movie theater, then describes the arrest.

12:59 am
NEW YORK

McGEE makes a few closing remarks on the tragedies that the Kennedy family has endured.

On Camera: The Presidential Seal.

STAR SPANGLED BANNER

1:02:17 am SIGN-OFF

Return to the White House

55

Saturday, Nov. 23, 1963

7:00 am
NEW YORK SIGN-ON

"TODAY" SHOW (Special Edition)

HUGH DOWNS, with the aid of film clips, recaps Friday's events, from the start of the motorcade in Dallas to the arrival of the Presidential jet in Washington last night.

7:20 am
ST. PATRICK'S CATHEDRAL, NEW YORK

FRANK BLAIR describes the interior of the cathedral, as the camera pans across the people waiting outside to attend an early mass for the dead. A memorial casket, draped with an American flag, stands in the middle aisle of the cathedral.

7:34 am
UNITED NATIONS

PAULINE FREDERICK: The UN was in session yesterday when the announcement of the President's death came in. President of the General Assembly Carlos Sosa Rodriguez asked all to rise for a minute of silence in memory of President Kennedy. The session was adjourned at the close of the silent tribute.

7:45 am
NEW YORK

BARBARA WALTERS: The streets of New York were deserted last night. Broadway theaters were closed. Radio City was closed. The only night club not deserted was the Stork Club, but the people there were like the people there on Christmas Eve, people with no home, no place to go. . . . The department stores stopped decorating. All the candles were lit in St. Patrick's Cathedral.

7:51 am
WASHINGTON, D.C.

AGRONSKY and historian Sidney Hyman discuss the effects of the death of a President, the disorder that sets in when the Vice President—who, strictly speaking, has not been chosen by the people—takes over as President. A country's history changes profoundly when an assassination takes place. Agronsky and Hyman list the successes and failures of Vice Presidents who have assumed the Presidential office through the death of a President.

8:01 am
NEW YORK

BLAIR: Prime Minister Douglas-Home of England plans to fly to Washington for the funeral of President Kennedy.

Saturday, Nov. 23, 1963

BLAIR: The body of the late President is in the East Room of the White House now. At 11 am this morning, President Johnson and Chief Justice Earl Warren will pay their respects at the casket of the late President.

8:03 am
DALLAS

MURPHY: Lee Oswald is still protesting his innocence.

Film: Lee Oswald asking for legal assistance.

MURPHY: No one knows if the assassination was an organized plot or whether Lee Oswald did it on his own. . . . Gov. Connally slept well last night. He has not yet been told of the President's death.

BLAIR: The body of the late President will lie in state from 10 am to 6 pm today.

8:14 am
WASHINGTON, D.C.

DICKERSON: The gates of the White House are closed now. Extreme security measures are being taken. President Johnson will go to the White House today to view the casket and to pay his respects to Mrs. Kennedy.

Film: President Johnson's home in the Spring Valley section of Washington, D.C.

8:16 am
VIA RELAY SATELLITE FROM LONDON

POPE PAUL VI: We are so deeply shocked over the death of this great statesman, the first Catholic President of the U.S. He was a great and good man.

8:38 am
ST. PATRICK'S CATHEDRAL

BLAIR describes the catafalque in the center aisle of the cathedral and comments on the other religious services to be held today.

8:43 am
LAFAYETTE PARK, WASHINGTON, D.C.

BRYSON RASH conducts on-the-street interviews. Two young men from Iran are "completely in sorrow"; they wept when they heard the news. Kennedy, they say, was well liked by the Iranian people.

On Camera: The White House door draped in black.

8:47 am
WASHINGTON, D.C.

AGRONSKY: President Johnson will come to the White House about 9 am to meet with Secretary of State Rusk.

8:50 am
NEW YORK

DOWNS: Throughout the land, people are mourning. All parties in Washington have been canceled. Embassy flags are at half-staff. In Chicago, night clubs are closed. Disneyland is closed, beauty pageants have been canceled, sports events, the Harvard-Yale game. . . . Many precautions had been taken in Dallas. The Secret Service always works with local police to screen out any dangerous person present in the city before the President arrives.

BLAIR: A solemn requiem mass will be said at St. Patrick's Cathedral at 10 am.

DOWNS: The stock market yesterday had its worst day since Black Monday, May 28, 1962.

BLAIR: In a news broadcast filled with attacks on the U.S., Red China gave its brief report of John F. Kennedy's death.

9:00 am
WHITE HOUSE

Tape: The casket lying in state in the East Room, draped with an American flag. Four large candles burn at each corner. An Honor Guard representing all the Armed Forces stands at attention.

VANOCUR: There will be two priests in attendance in here all day. Television cameras were allowed in the East Room for 15 minutes this morning by Mrs. Kennedy.

On Camera: The Honor Guard salutes the casket and solemnly changes guard.

VANOCUR: Mrs. Kennedy is in the White House, but the whereabouts of the Kennedy children are unknown.

9:06 am
WASHINGTON, D.C.

SEN. JOHN TOWER (D-Tex.) reads a letter written to him several years ago by Lee Oswald, requesting the Senator's help in returning to the U.S. from the Soviet Union. Sen. Tower states that his secretary remembered Oswald's name and produced the letter from his files yesterday.

REP. HALE BOGGS (R-La.): The whole country is suffering from shock. We are not a country of violence, and the notion of an American

Saturday, Nov. 23, 1963

President being assassinated is abhorrent to everyone. . . . An awesome responsibility rests on President Johnson now. Rep. Charles Halleck, the House Minority Leader, was the first to speak at the meeting of Congressional leaders. "Mr. President," he said, "you have our full support." Sen. Dirksen, the Senate Minority Leader, then spoke up and said that we all would work together for the country. At the close of the meeting, we all said, "God bless you, Mr. President."

REP. GERALD K. FORD, JR. (R-Mich.): There is a whole-hearted and sincere effort to stand by the new President. No one can believe what happened yesterday, the shock is so great. Our late President understood the Congressional process better than any President of recent times. The maximum effort will be exerted to support the new President.

SEN. TOWER: Partisanship should be buried for a while in order to give full support to President Johnson.

REP. BOGGS: President Johnson will make a good President. I have been as close to Lyndon Johnson as I was to President Kennedy. Any man who reaches this ultimate spot understands fully what the office stands for. Johnson is superbly qualified to be President of the U.S. His reactions will be individual and personal, but he has the basic sense of what our country is. We shall all miss the great humanity of our late President. He never asked everyone to agree with him all the time. He was an intellectual—and a fine, warm human being.

9:20 am
NEW YORK
Photographs: Mrs. Rose Kennedy, mother of the late President, attending 7:00 am Mass today at Hyannis Port; Premier Khrushchev at the American Embassy in Moscow.

DOWNS: Premier Khrushchev will send Andrei Gromyko to attend the funeral.

DOWNS: Lee Oswald has been charged with the murder of the Dallas policeman. He has not confessed.

9:22 am
ST. PATRICK'S CATHEDRAL NEW YORK

MSGR. TIMOTHY FLYNN (Archdiocese of N.Y.): I first heard the news on radio and television. At first I did not believe it; I hoped he would survive the wound. The cathedral has been filled all afternoon. There was a public recitation of the rosary for President Kennedy, and special prayers in the evening. Tomorrow, at 10 am, Bishop McGuire will offer a mass for the dead. A catafalque simulating the coffin of the dead person will be a part of the ceremony. Black vestments will be worn. We expect a huge crowd at this mass.

9:27 am
OLD STATE DEPT. BLDG. WASHINGTON, D.C. (ACROSS FROM WHITE HOUSE)

On Camera: Lyndon Johnson walking toward the old State Department building with his aides.

SCHERER: Lyndon Johnson has his office in that building. He was at the White House earlier today.

9:30 am
NEW YORK

DOWNS: President Johnson is the first President from the South since Andrew Johnson, who succeeded Lincoln.

9:35 am
WASHINGTON, D.C.

REP. CARL ALBERT (D-Okla.): I haven't yet recovered from the shock. I saw President Kennedy not 48 hours ago, and he had more life in him than anybody. . . . Lyndon Johnson possesses excellent qualifications for the Presidency. There are fewer differences than similarities between John F. Kennedy and Lyndon B. Johnson. Like President Kennedy, Johnson loves political battles and the game of politics. . . . People idolized the late President, but he always gave back even more warmth than he received. . . . President Johnson knows everyone in Congress well. Every man, Democrat and Republican, has pledged his support.

9:41 am
ST. PATRICK'S CATHEDRAL

BLAIR: People are entering the cathedral. The sky is overcast.

Mrs. Rose Kennedy

Saturday, Nov. 23, 1963

9:43 am
UNITED NATIONS
FREDERICK: There is silence here. Yesterday, after hearing the news, the delegates stood in hushed groups. The blue UN flag was lowered to half-staff. There will be no business conducted here until after the funeral. After the funeral, there will be a memorial. The people at the UN remember John F. Kennedy's two appearances at the General Assembly, and his challenges for peace.

9:47 am
ANDREWS
AIR FORCE
BASE
KAPLOW: Many officials will be landing here, arriving for the funeral. Last night, six members of the Cabinet returned here.

9:52 am
DALLAS
MURPHY: Gov. Connally's condition is improving. He has been told that the President is dead.

MURPHY discusses the assassination with Dr. Malcolm Perry, first physician to treat the President. A blackboard diagram shows the position of the Presidential car and the angle of the bullets. By turning, Gov. Connally saved his life, for the bullet that would have otherwise penetrated his heart, only struck his chest. Dr. Perry explains that there was never any hope of saving the President.

10:06 am
OLD STATE
DEPT. BLDG.
SCHERER: President Johnson is using his old office in the old State Department building until after the funeral. He says he felt as if the whole world had fallen in on him. . . . John McCone, head of the CIA, has conferred with President Johnson. . . . It is now raining heavily in Washington.

10:11 am
NEW YORK
McGEE: The Dallas police are convinced that Lee Oswald is guilty, but they still have no confession or admission of guilt. . . . President Kennedy's ailing father has been told of his son's death.

10:12 am
DALLAS
CITY HALL
PETTIT interviews Deputy Police Chief M. W. Stevenson.

STEVENSON: An investigation into the assassination is fully underway. Eyewitnesses are being sought. So far no one has been found who actually saw Oswald pull the trigger. Oswald was jailed on a charge of murdering President Kennedy; there is no charge on the books for assassination as such. Oswald is being held in jail on the fourth floor. He continues to deny that he killed President Kennedy.

10:17 am
WHITE HOUSE

Tape: The casket in the East Room.

VANOCUR (voice over): The Kennedy family will view the casket at 10:30 am today. Former President Eisenhower and former President Truman will be here tomorrow.

10:30 am
ST. PATRICK'S
CATHEDRAL
NEW YORK

On Camera: The consecration of the mass offered for the late President.

10:46 am
WHITE HOUSE

SCHERER: One by one the cars are pulling up to the portico. Secretary of Labor Willard Wirtz has just entered the White House.

10:49 am
NEW YORK

McGEE: Oswald still insists he did not kill the President. The paraffin tests proved positive—Oswald did fire a gun during the last 24 hours. Dallas Police Chief Jesse Curry says Oswald has been charged with murdering the President and Dallas policeman J. D. Tippit.

RYAN: Sen. Edward Kennedy has gone to Hyannis Port to be with Mrs. Rose Kennedy. A neurologist is attending Mr. Joseph Kennedy.

10:54 am
DALLAS

PETTIT interviews Dallas Police Chief Jesse Curry.

CURRY: The results of the paraffin test are positive, proving that the suspect, Lee Harvey Oswald, had fired a gun in the last 24 hours. The fingerprints on the rifle were only partial and cannot be identified as Oswald's.

10:56 am
WHITE HOUSE

VANOCUR: Many Senate leaders are meeting today with President Johnson in the Executive Office building (the old State Department building) across the street from

Mrs. Robert F. Kennedy

Saturday, Nov. 23, 1963

the White House. President Johnson is in his office with Presidential adviser McGeorge Bundy and others.

10:59 am
ATLANTA, GA.

Tape: Interview with Dr. Martin Luther King.

DR. KING: President Kennedy's Civil Rights Bill was the best we have had from any President. Unmerited suffering is redemptive, a price paid to free our children from a spiritual death. When a cause is right, we must have courage. When a man lives constantly under the threat of death, he becomes immune to fear after a while.

11:04 am
WASHINGTON NATIONAL CATHEDRAL WASHINGTON, D.C.

On Camera: Memorial services for the late President Kennedy, conducted by the Very Rev. Francis B. Sayre, Dean of the Cathedral.

11:29 am
WHITE HOUSE

SCHERER: The Chief Justices are now entering the White House to view the casket.

GORALSKI: French President Charles de Gaulle will fly here tomorrow, as will Britain's Prince Philip and Prime Minister Douglas-Home.... The rain is pouring down.

REP. CHARLES HALLECK (R-Ind.): We have paid our respects to a great man.

REP. LESLIE C. ARENDS (R-Ill.): Congressional leaders have pledged their support to the new President.

SCHERER: Members of the late President's Cabinet will be arriving shortly.... Former President Eisenhower is scheduled to meet with President Johnson today.

11:36 am
DALLAS POLICE HDQ.

On Camera: Lee Oswald being taken from the elevator to the homicide bureau.

PETTIT: There is a tremendous crush of reporters around Lee Oswald.... He is being held without bond.

CURRY: FBI men, Secret Service police and Capt. Will Fritz of the homicide bureau are all participating in the questioning of Lee Oswald.

11:38 am
NEW YORK

McGEE: When Gov. Connally was Secretary of the Navy, Lee Oswald wrote him a letter asking him to reverse his dishonorable discharge from the Marine Corps. Connally refused.

11:41 am
WHITE HOUSE

SCHERER: It is reported that President and Mrs. Johnson and former President Eisenhower have gone across the street to President Johnson's office for a meeting. . . . Mrs. Jacqueline Kennedy and the two Kennedy children visited the casket this morning. Mrs. Kennedy was heavily veiled. The two children clung to their mother's skirts.

On Camera: Former Secretary of State Christian Herter and Under Secretary of State Averell Harriman arrive at the White House. Sen. Hubert Humphrey and CIA Director John McCone leave. Mr. and Mrs. Sargent Shriver arrive, followed by Under Secretary of State George Ball, Ambassador-at-large Llewellyn Thompson, and Esther Peterson. . . . A car bearing President Johnson heads toward St. John's Church where a memorial service for the late President will be held.

MUELLER (voice over): President Johnson is a member of the Congregational Christian Church. . . . The National Cathedral in Washington held a memorial service from 11 am to noon today.

12:41 pm
NEW YORK

RYAN: Lee Oswald, the man accused of murdering the President, was interviewed by the FBI a week ago. According to Police Chief Curry the FBI did not notify the Dallas police of Oswald's presence in Dallas.

12:43 pm
DALLAS
POLICE HDQ.

CURRY: We have no knowledge of Oswald's presence in the city. They—the FBI—didn't warn us of his presence, although they usually do. They usually let us know when any communist sympathizers and subversives are in the city. Oswald is known to have brought a large package to work with him

Christian Herter

yesterday morning—believed to be his rifle—and he was up on the sixth floor around noon. When a police officer saw him in the building, the manager of the Depository told the officer, "He's all right—he works here."

PETTIT and CURRY discuss the fact that Oswald wrote a letter to Gov. Connally.

CURRY: Perhaps Gov. Connally was his real target. Or maybe he wanted to kill both men.

12:50 pm
WHITE HOUSE

SCHERER: Plans have been made for President de Gaulle and Foreign Minister Couve de Murville of France to attend the funeral. Japanese Prime Minister Ikeda will also attend.

VANOCUR: President Kennedy's White House office is in a state of chaos.

MUELLER: There was no involvement of the Soviet Union or any other foreign power in the shooting.

12:59 pm
VIA RELAY
SATELLITE
FROM
WEST BERLIN

MAYOR WILLY BRANDT: On behalf of the people of Berlin, I would like to express our sorrow at the death of President Kennedy. The work of his life must be carried on. The goals have not changed. I ask the Lord's blessing for President Johnson.

1:03 pm
NEW YORK

McGEE: A second man has been arrested. . . . A justice of the peace issued a search warrant to enter Oswald's rented room. Oswald was a Marine at Camp Pendleton, Calif., and a fairly expert marksman. He called himself a Marxist. Police Chief Curry says that Oswald later made no distinction between the terms Marxist and communist.

1:05 pm
KANSAS
CITY, MISSOURI

Film: President Harry S. Truman's statement on the assassination.

◀

PRESIDENT TRUMAN: I am touched beyond words. The death of President Kennedy is a personal loss and a loss to the country. He was an able President, one the people loved and trusted.

1:07 pm
NEW YORK

McGEE: President Kennedy never knew what hit him. In effect, he was dead on arrival at the hospital—his pulse was gone. There was never any hope of survival.

Tape: President John F. Kennedy's speech at the Berlin Wall, June 26, 1963.

RYAN: President Johnson is attending memorial services for the late President.

McGEE: Lee Oswald has been formally charged with the murder of President Kennedy. Paraffin tests on the side of Oswald's face proved that he had indeed fired a rifle.

Film (no sound): President Johnson's activities today; the private services at his home; the meetings at the White House and the Executive Office Building.

1:21 pm
WHITE HOUSE
VANOCUR reads excerpts from President Johnson's first proclamation (his first official act as President), which he will deliver live later this afternoon.

1:23 pm
WASHINGTON, D.C.
MUELLER: Cardinal Cushing of Boston will celebrate the funeral mass. . . .
A prayer for President Johnson was said at St. John's Church earlier today.

1:26 pm
WHITE HOUSE
◀ **SCHERER:** President Kennedy's rocking chairs have already been removed from his office.

DICKERSON describes President Johnson's office in the Executive Office building, noting that he especially likes Texas landscape paintings by Porfirio Salinas.

DICKERSON: President Truman will arrive at 2:10 pm. . . . Mrs. Roswell Gilpatric told me that President Kennedy telephoned her husband a few days ago, congratulating him on the good job he had performed testifying before a rather hostile subcommittee investigating the TFX defense contract.

MUELLER: The Defense Department will not change under the new President. The role of the military in space will be reviewed.

Saturday, Nov. 23, 1963

1:36 pm
DALLAS POLICE HDQ.
PETTIT: Oswald still refuses to confess to the murder or to take a lie-detector test.

1:38 pm
NEW YORK
Tape Repeat: Agronsky relates Adlai Stevenson's misgivings about the President's trip to Dallas.

McGEE: Oswald refuses to take a lie-detector test. . . . The place of the Kennedy burial has not yet been decided.

Tape: President Kennedy's visit to Ireland, June 1963. The President speaks of his proud heritage, of his grandfather who left Ireland to come to the U.S. He tells a story of the Irishman who returned to Ireland from the U.S. with a picture of the White House and told his relatives that it was his summer home.

McGEE: Mrs. Kennedy and her two children viewed the casket earlier today. Mrs. Kennedy has told her children that their father is dead. . . . Mrs. Joseph Kennedy attended two masses today. Mr. Joseph Kennedy has been told of his son's death. . . . The Rotunda of the Capitol has been roped off in preparation for public viewing of the casket.

1:50 pm
WHITE HOUSE
Tape: Casket in East Room. Mourners include 75 members of the family, and close friends of the late President.

1:52 pm
NEW YORK
McGEE: The Cabinet has been asked to stay on. . . . Aldous Huxley, the novelist, died last night. . . . President Truman is due to arrive in Washington soon.

McGEE: It is raining in Washington, D.C. . . . So much history is taking place in so short a time.

Tape: Excerpt from President Kennedy's address at American University, June 10, 1963, in which he asked that world tensions be eased as a first step in the direction of a nuclear test ban treaty negotiation. (A limited test ban treaty went into effect Oct. 10, 1963.)

STATION IDENTIFICATION

2:00 pm
DALLAS
POLICE HDQ.

PETTIT interviews Dallas District Attorney Henry Wade.

WADE: There is sufficient evidence to convict Lee Oswald, but I cannot comment before the trial. The case will be presented to the Grand Jury within the next two weeks. We will ask the death penalty.

2:02 pm
WASHINGTON,
D.C.

Film: Eisenhower arriving at Washington's National Airport to meet with President Johnson.

2:07 pm
NEW YORK

RYAN: Under the Constitution, Lyndon Johnson may run for two terms after completing Kennedy's unfinished term.

2:27 pm
WHITE HOUSE

On Camera: The arrival of dignitaries at East Room. President Johnson is seen with McGeorge Bundy and George Reedy. President Truman arrives and is greeted by Sargent Shriver and Angier Biddle Duke; he goes directly to the East Room.

Tape Repeat: Dignitaries arriving at the White House.

3:00 pm
ANDREWS
AIR FORCE
BASE

KAPLOW: Planes have been arriving here all afternoon.

GOV. ROSS BARNETT (D-Miss.): The people of Mississippi were extremely sorry to hear of the President's assassination. It was a cowardly act. The people of our state are in deep grief; the flags are flying at half-staff. Upon hearing of the tragic event, I immediately wired Mrs. Kennedy and Gov. Connally. . . . President Johnson is well known in Mississippi. . . . Every Mississippian is deeply grieved.

3:06 pm
WHITE HOUSE

On Camera: Dignitaries continue to arrive at White House. President Johnson is seen crossing the street to his office. NBC reporters Dickerson and Rash discuss the Cabinet meeting, which began with a short prayer and lasted 25 minutes. Johnson asked the present Cabinet to continue serving.

3:14 pm
DALLAS
POLICE HDQ.

PETTIT: Police have uncovered several details in connection with the suspect Lee Oswald.

Saturday, Nov. 23, 1963

It is known that he left the Texas School Book Depository building after the assassination took place, headed for home, changed his clothes, and went to a movie theater. A cab driver and a bus driver have been located who recognized Lee Oswald.

CAPT. FRITZ: This man Oswald killed the President. We have a cinch case against him.

3:16 pm
NEW YORK

McGEE: The FBI, I am told, interviewed Oswald a few days before the President came to Dallas. People who knew Oswald said he was a bookish introvert–always a "loner." After reading Das Kapital he felt converted to communism. Oswald joined the Marines and twice faced possible court martial. He never rose above Pfc. In the Marines he acted aloof–a lonely boy. His Marine career ended in 1957. Oswald was placed on inactive reserve with a dishonorable discharge. He then traveled to Russia, claiming he was a Marxist. He turned in his U.S. passport and affirmed his allegiance to the Soviet Union. He married a Russian woman. While in Russia he wrote a letter to Sen. John Tower of Texas asking for help in returning to the U.S.; Tower referred his letter to the State Department.

3:30 pm
WASHINGTON, D.C.

DICKERSON: When former President Harry Truman came to pay his final respects to the late President Kennedy, he also visited with Mrs. Kennedy.

MUELLER: Elie Abel reports that a grave site has been chosen in Arlington Cemetery.

3:36 pm
NEW YORK

McGEE: A jury must be chosen for the Oswald trial. This will cause considerable difficulty.

3:43 pm
WHITE HOUSE

SCHERER (voice over) names some of the foreign dignitaries expected to arrive tomorrow.

MUELLER: The President's body is now in repose in the White House. Governors and Congressmen are calling to pay their respects.

Captain Will Fritz

Ambassador Henry Cabot Lodge

3:48 pm
NEW YORK

RYAN: Robert Kennedy went today to Arlington Cemetery to select the grave site.

RYAN: President Johnson today called President Kennedy "a good and great man." He asked the Cabinet and the ambassadors to stay on; he called for no resignations. In 35 minutes he will meet with former President Truman.

4:01 pm
WHITE HOUSE

RASH: The diplomatic corps will be arriving within the hour.

MUELLER: There will be a high mass Monday, Cardinal Cushing officiating.

4:03 pm
NEW YORK

RYAN lists names of world leaders who will attend the funeral. He recalls Khrushchev's reaction to the news, and the Soviet leader's subsequent message to his people.

STATION IDENTIFICATION

4:09 pm
WASHINGTON, D.C.

DICKERSON: Justice Goldberg wept when he heard the news. He is on his way to see President Johnson.

SCHERER: At 1:00 pm tomorrow, the body of the late President will leave the White House for the Capitol building.

4:14 pm
NEW YORK

RYAN: This is the second night the people of West Berlin have been mourning the death of John F. Kennedy. . . . At 4:40 pm today, President Johnson will address the nation.

4:17 pm
WASHINGTON, D.C.

ABERNETHY interviews Gov. Abraham Ribicoff (D-Conn.).

GOV. RIBICOFF: I was on the floor of the Senate when I heard the news. . . . I feel that the Kennedy philosophy and the Kennedy politics will be the Johnson credo, too. Lyndon Johnson is aware of all the personal problems of the Cabinet members. In the months ahead, the present Cabinet will work shoulder to shoulder with the President. Even though Robert Kennedy and Lyndon Johnson have been antagonists, they have had and will continue to have respect for each other, and Robert Kennedy will, no doubt, continue as Attorney General.

Saturday, Nov. 23, 1963

4:25 pm
NEW YORK
McGEE: John F. Kennedy's father Joe is one of the wealthiest men in the country, with an estimated $300,000,000 to his name.

4:28 pm
WASHINGTON, D.C.
ABERNETHY: The body of the President will lie in state in the Capitol Rotunda tomorrow. Later tomorrow afternoon, the public will be admitted.

4:30 pm
NEW YORK
McGEE: The court of Queen Elizabeth has gone into mourning for a week. The flag of France is flying at half-staff. Mrs. Kennedy has received messages of condolence from—among others—Premier Khrushchev, British Prime Minister Douglas-Home, Canadian Prime Minister Lester Pearson, and UN Secretary General U Thant.

4:51 pm
WASHINGTON, D.C.
PRESIDENT LYNDON BAINES JOHNSON: John Fitzgerald Kennedy, 35th President of the United States, has been taken from us by an act which outrages decent men everywhere.

He upheld the faith of our Fathers, which is freedom for all men. He broadened the frontiers of that faith, and backed it with the energy and the courage which are the mark of the Nation that he led.

A man of wisdom, strength and peace, he molded and moved the power of our Nation in the service of a world of growing liberty and order. All who love freedom will mourn his death.

As he did not shrink from his responsibilities, but welcomed them, so he would not have us shrink from carrying on his work beyond this hour of national tragedy.

He said it himself: "The energy, the faith, the devotion which we bring to this endeavor will light our country and all who serve it, and the glow from that fire can truly light the world."

Now, therefore, I, Lyndon B. Johnson, President of the United States of America, do appoint Monday next, Nov. 25, the day of the funeral service of President Kennedy,

London in mourning

to be a day of national mourning throughout
the United States. I earnestly recommend
the people to assemble on that day in their
respective places of divine worship, there to
bow down in submission to the will of
Almighty God, and to pay their homage
of love and reverence to the memory of a
great and good man. I invite the people
of the world who share our grief to join us in
this day of mourning and rededication.

In witness whereof, I have hereunto
set my hand and cause the Seal of the
United States of America to be affixed.

Done at the City of Washington this
twenty-third day of November in the year
of our Lord nineteen hundred and sixty-three,
and of the Independence of the United States
of America the one hundred and eighty-eighth.

4:55 pm **VANOCUR:** That was President Johnson's
first formal address to the American people....
All the effects of John F. Kennedy have
been removed from the oval office.

MUELLER: President Johnson has been
somewhat in the background today; all focus
is on the White House and Mrs. Kennedy.

5:04 pm
WHITE HOUSE **ABEL:** Diplomats and dignitaries are filing
slowly past the casket inside the East Room.

5:05 pm
WASHINGTON,
D.C. **BRINKLEY:** Washington is full of traffic
jams today, as thousands are converging on
the city to pay their last respects to the
late President.

5:16 pm
WHITE HOUSE **ABEL:** Among the foreign dignitaries who
will attend the funeral are French President
Charles de Gaulle, Prince Philip of England,
and West Berlin Mayor Willy Brandt.

5:20 pm
NEW YORK **HUNTLEY:** Sen. Edward Kennedy informed
his father, Joseph Kennedy, that President
Kennedy had been slain. Because of ill
health, Joseph Kennedy is not expected to
attend his son's funeral.

HUNTLEY: Gov. John Connally, recovering

Saturday, Nov. 23, 1963

in a Dallas hospital, has been told that the President is dead. He had suspected the worst. Connally is making good progress, and his mind is clear. . . . Nineteen sixty-two was the crucial year in the Kennedy administration, the year of the Mississippi integration crisis and the Cuban crisis. . . . Kennedy was President two years, ten months and two days.

5:27 pm Tape Repeat: "After Two Years . . . A Conversation with the President." (Originally ◄ broadcast Dec. 17, 1962.) Sander Vanocur of NBC, Bill Lawrence of ABC, and George Herman of CBS interview President Kennedy in his White House office, reviewing his first two years in office.

6:27 pm
WASHINGTON, D.C. BRINKLEY: President Johnson will address a joint session of Congress on Wednesday, Nov. 27. The address will be carried live on television at 12:30 pm.

6:28 pm
WHITE HOUSE SCHERER: A press conference with Pierre Salinger has just ended. President Kennedy will be buried in Arlington National Cemetery.

6:29 pm
WASHINGTON, D.C. Film: Robert Kennedy, Robert McNamara and others choosing the grave site. ◄

BRINKLEY: The funeral service will be held Monday at noon at St. Matthew's Cathedral, the largest Catholic church in Washington, D.C.

Film: St. Matthew's Cathedral.

6:32 pm
NEW YORK HUNTLEY: John, Jr., son of the late President, was heard to say, "My father was killed by a bad man. I don't have anyone to play with." John, Jr. cannot understand why he can't go into the Oval Room, the President's office. Caroline comprehends the tragedy. Mrs. Jacqueline Kennedy has tried to hold up bravely through all of this. Those close to her say that the full impact has yet to hit her.

6:35 pm
HOUSTON Tape Repeat: An informal interview with Lyndon Johnson on his ranch west of Austin, Texas, held Sept. 27, 1963. Seated at a picnic table outside his home,

Lyndon Johnson speaks of his early life—
how his family came to settle in this part of
the country, how he attended and taught
school here. He talks of his decision to
accept the Vice Presidential slot on the 1960
ticket. He enjoys being Vice President
of the country he loves, and believes the
"ugly American" image is "just a lot of bunk."
"If we prevail," he says, "it is for one reason,
and that is our form of government. Our
economic system is the best ever devised. The
capitalist, the manager and the worker all
fit together in the picture. I'm not afraid of
our future. I'm not one who hates. We will
prevail. We have a lot to protect and
preserve, a lot to be proud of—and a little
to be ashamed of. Our biggest problem is
learning to get along with rest of the world.
Our American system is not the most
perfect system, but it is the best."

6:58 pm NEAL gives an assessment of President
LOS ANGELES Johnson's feelings about the space program.

Film: A mass being said for President
Kennedy; a cannon being fired at a California
army base; an empty Los Angeles Coliseum.

7:03 pm HUNTLEY: The first critical Pravda editorial
NEW YORK has appeared. It objects to the character-
ization of Lee Oswald as a communist.

STATION IDENTIFICATION

7:06 pm BRINKLEY: Rose Kennedy, mother of the
WASHINGTON, late President, will attend the funeral.
D.C. Mrs. Jacqueline Kennedy has indicated she
will walk behind the caisson bearing the
body of the late President from the White
House to St. Matthew's Cathedral.

Film: President Johnson in his office
with President Truman. ◀

7:11 pm HUNTLEY: The Dallas police have stated
NEW YORK publicly that there is no doubt in their minds
that Lee Oswald is the murderer of the
President.

Saturday, Nov. 23, 1963

7:15 pm
DALLAS

H. LOUIS NICHOLS (President of the Dallas Bar Association): I visited with Oswald in his cell. He indicated he wanted a lawyer named John J. Abt of New York, or one from the American Civil Liberties Union, who, as he put it, "believes in the same things I do." He was not defiant, but he definitely did not want a Dallas attorney to represent him. The Oswald family is endeavoring to get in contact with Abt. I believe Oswald will get a fair trial in Dallas.

MURPHY: Lee Harvey Oswald is being moved once more—into the interrogation room for further questioning. It is difficult to see him for all the reporters and photographers gathered here. The Dallas police are calling this an iron-clad case—they are positive he shot and killed the President.

7:24 pm
NEW ORLEANS

Film: The Oswalds' apartment in New Orleans. Jim Kempt interviews the landlady, who says that the Oswald couple caused no trouble during their stay.

LANDLADY: They were quiet and cooperative, and they left promptly when they found themselves unable to pay the rent. A car with a Texas license plate arrived one day— the same car that had brought them to New Orleans—and off they went.

KEMPT interviews the owner of the local grocery store.

GROCER: Mrs. Oswald came in once in a while for a loaf of bread. Lee Oswald came into the store twice. One time he tried to borrow money. The other time he asked me to turn on the TV set so he could watch something. I told him no both times.

7:31 pm
DALLAS
POLICE HDQ.

PETTIT interviews Police Chief Curry, who states that Oswald will soon be transferred from the jail. There is no information on the accomplices, if indeed any exist.

Film: Lee Oswald asking for a clean shirt.
Film: Oswald's wife, child and mother visiting him at the jail. ◀

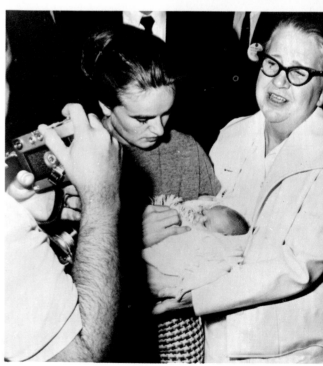

Film: Bill Seymour interviews Rev. Oscar Huber, the priest who administered the last rites to the late President Kennedy.

FATHER HUBER: When the last rites were given, a sheet was over the President's head. No one knew whether he was alive or dead. I talked briefly with Mrs. Kennedy, who was present every moment. She thanked me for taking care of the President's spiritual needs. Then I recited some prayers with Mrs. Kennedy. Every person present was in a state of shock. Mrs. Kennedy appeared composed—almost paralyzed. She was not crying. She spoke very softly at times.

7:45 pm
NEW YORK

HUNTLEY: Citizens of Dallas have placed flowers on the lawn near the spot where President Kennedy was fatally shot.

Tape: Lyndon Johnson's 4th of July speech on civil rights. ("Some say now. Some say never. Let's say all together.")

7:47 pm
WASHINGTON, D.C.

SCHERER interviews Sen. Humphrey on the question of what kind of President Lyndon Johnson will be.

SEN. HUMPHREY: Lyndon Johnson will make a very forceful President. He is active, hardworking—a great patriot. Johnson worked closely with the late President and feels strongly about human equality. Some people are concerned about the transition, but our Constitution provides for this situation very well, and in this particular case we are especially lucky to have such a good man follow in the steps of a truly great President.

VANOCUR: Lyndon Johnson will follow the policy laid down by John F. Kennedy. He will have his Southern origins to fight against, for although his record in Congress has proved differently, people still think of him as a sectional politician.

ABEL: Johnson will make no great changes in the Cabinet. He has no great experience in foreign affairs and will lean heavily on

Saturday, Nov. 23, 1963

Cabinet knowledge. Most likely, he will follow Kennedy's policies. We will have to wait and see what kind of leadership these tragic events have given us.

AGRONSKY: This leadership takes courage. Political courage is difficult, but Johnson has shown it in the past—for example, his vote against off-shore oil legislation.

DICKERSON: Johnson is proud of his humble background and has always shown a kindness to those not so important.
He is a thoughtful man, but he can be tough.

VANOCUR, AGRONSKY, ABEL and DICKERSON discuss Lyndon Johnson in relationship to past Presidents. Kennedy and Eisenhower, they agree, had glamor; Johnson is more like Truman—hard-working and sincere. They discuss Johnson's record in Congress, his rise to Senate Majority Leader. They compare his folksiness to Premier Khrushchev's.

AGRONSKY: Some people tried to dissuade Lyndon Johnson from accepting the Vice Presidency. He wanted it, and he accepted it, knowing that John F. Kennedy was boss and that he, Lyndon Johnson, would be taking a back seat.

BRINKLEY: As President, Lyndon Johnson so far has displayed great vigor. He has scheduled a high-echelon meeting tomorrow. The cooperation being shown within the government is outstanding.

STATION IDENTIFICATION

8:25 pm
NEW YORK

HUNTLEY: Attorney General Robert Kennedy spent most of the day at the White House.

8:26 pm
DALLAS POLICE HDQ.

PETTIT: Two new pieces of evidence have turned up.

CURRY: The FBI has just informed us that they've found a letter received by a mail-order house in Chicago for the purchase of the rifle which is believed to be the one that killed the President. The handwriting on the order is Lee Oswald's. The order is

Robert Kennedy with two of his children

78

dated March 20, 1963. Photographs have also been found which show Oswald holding this rifle. The name on the return address was A. Hidell, and the gun cost $12.78.

Tape: Lee Oswald in the third floor corridor of the Dallas jail.

8:31 pm
NEW YORK

HUNTLEY: Authorities report that Oswald was confident when accused and when confronted with the photographs mentioned, but slightly shaken when the authorities left.

Film: West Berlin memorial parade for John F. Kennedy. West Berlin Mayor Willy Brandt addresses the crowd.

MAYOR BRANDT: This square will be officially renamed for the late President. Students will demonstrate in his honor, for they especially feel that this tragedy that befell us all is a most serious one. . . . When Lyndon Johnson came to West Berlin, he remained here six days after the Wall was erected. The people of West Berlin appreciated his coming to pledge his support.

HUNTLEY: Oswald has admitted to being a communist, although the Communist Party the world over is disavowing Oswald. . . . Thirty Irish soldiers are arriving from Ireland to serve as an honor escort at the funeral of President Kennedy.

HUNTLEY: Even in her sorrow, Mrs. Jacqueline Kennedy has offered to help Mrs. Johnson in any way she can.

8:41 pm
WASHINGTON, D.C.

BRINKLEY: The President of the United States was killed by a punk with a mail-order rifle.

8:42 pm
CAPITOL

BRINKLEY (voice over): Workmen are busy reconstructing the catafalque used after the assassination of President Lincoln. The casket containing the body of John F. Kennedy will rest on this catafalque. Four President's bodies have lain in state at the Rotunda.

9:13 pm
NEW YORK

HUNTLEY tells how the police officer who apprehended Oswald in the movie theater

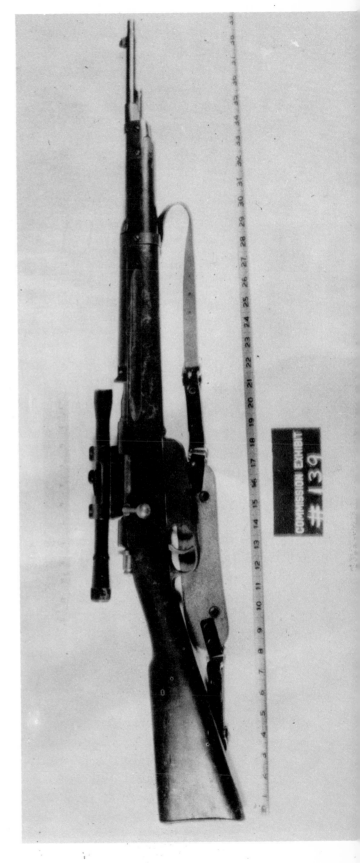

79

Saturday, Nov. 23, 1963

received the order to arrest him. Huntley
also reads a telegram to Frank McGee from
Akron, Ohio, suggesting that in lieu of
flowers, contributions be sent to the widow
of J. D. Tippit, the policeman slain yesterday
in Dallas.

STATION IDENTIFICATION

9:16 pm
WASHINGTON,
D.C.

BRINKLEY: President Johnson will address
Congress at 12:30 pm Wednesday. The
address will be televised.

Tape: President Truman's arrival in
Washington; his statement on the death of
President Kennedy; and his meeting with
President Johnson.

Tape: President Johnson leaving his office
for home.

BRINKLEY: There is no time set for the
change of households. The Johnsons will
continue to live in their own home for a while.

9:35 pm
NEW YORK

HUNTLEY: Oswald has requested that John
Abt of New York defend him. Abt was
interviewed tonight and says he has not been
asked to defend Oswald so far, and would be
unable to do so if asked, because of the
cases he already has pending.

9:37 pm
WASHINGTON,
D.C.

BRINKLEY reads telegrams from Rep. Claude
Pepper (D-Fla.) and Rep. James Roosevelt
(D-Calif.) indicating they will ask Congress
to award the Congressional Medal of Honor
to President Kennedy. . . . The Secret Service
has indicated they will tighten their security.
The Secret Service has always operated
under great stress, fearing an event like the
one which happened yesterday.

9:52 pm
NEW YORK

HUNTLEY: There will be no postal service
Monday. In New York, investment houses will
be closed on Monday; schools, movie
theaters, nightclubs, stores, the Port of
New York will all shut down. The city will be
as quiet as it was the day President
Kennedy died.

Greeting Anastas Mikoyan

Sargent Shriver

President Eisenhower

Mayor Robert F. Wagner

Senator Margaret Chase Smith

Saturday, Nov. 23, 1963

9:55 pm
WASHINGTON, D.C.
BRINKLEY: It is confirmed that the rifle in the hands of the authorities is the murder weapon. Sen. Dodd of Connecticut has pressed for legislation to curb the sale of firearms by mail-order houses. Fidel Castro spoke tonight and said that Cuba may face a worse fate with Johnson as President than it did with Kennedy. Louis Lomax urged Negroes all over the country to stop demonstrating until after the first of the year. The body of the late President will rest in the Rotunda of the Capitol after it is taken from the White House.

10:00 pm
NEW YORK
HUNTLEY: Some of the foreign dignitaries who will attend the funeral will remain in Washington to meet briefly with the new President.

10:03 pm
WASHINGTON, D.C.
BRINKLEY comments on the trick golf club that President Kennedy owned. He then mentions a conversation that he and Huntley once had with the new President, and comments on Johnson's consuming interest in politics. Brinkley also mentions Sen. Mike Mansfield and his position in the Democratic Party.

10:08 pm
NEW YORK
HUNTLEY gives his personal opinion of President Kennedy, referring to his absolute poise and confidence, his ability to retain and quote statistics, and his self-control.

10:10 pm
WASHINGTON, D.C.
BRINKLEY: Kennedy did show controlled anger when the steel industry raised its prices. He would not tone down his statement even when Arthur Goldberg, then Secretary of Labor, and Willard Wirtz expressed concern at the strong language. Kennedy eventually made his speech at a press conference and it turned out four times as strong as the one he had prepared. It was one of the few times he showed his anger publicly; he was really mad. However, during the Cuban crisis his manner was unemotional, detached and serene.

6.5 ITALIAN CARBINE
Late military issue. Only 40" over all. Weighs 7 lbs. Shows only slig use, test-fired and head spaced, rea for shooting. Turned-down bolt, shot, clip fed, rear sight. $12⁷
thumb safety.
C20-1196 ....
C20-750. Carbine with brand new scope—¾" dia. (illustrated) $19.9

Steel strike press conference

82

10:15 pm HUNTLEY recalls his last interview with the
NEW YORK President, Sept. 1962. The interview was held
in Washington at the President's White
House office; Brinkley was also present. One
of the questions related to South Vietnam.
The President answered, then asked if he
could retape his reply. Huntley says that
while the first answer was good, the second
was even better.

BRINKLEY: President Kennedy will be buried
in Arlington National Cemetery.

Film Repeat: Robert Kennedy and others
selecting a grave site; the catafalque being
erected in the Rotunda; St. Matthew's
Cathedral, site of Monday's funeral.

BRINKLEY: The body of the late President
will be brought to the Capitol from the White
House by horse-drawn caisson. Irish soldiers
have been invited to take part. The family
has requested that no flowers be sent, but
this request has been widely ignored. The
casket will be closed at all times. NBC will
be in Washington to cover all the events as
they unfold tomorrow. An unprecedented
number of people are expected to arrive in
Washington tomorrow.

10:46 pm HUNTLEY reads some of the British press
NEW YORK reaction to the assassination.

HUNTLEY: Lee Oswald is being held in a
Dallas jail. . . . Numerous foreign dignitaries
and heads of state will attend the funeral. . . .
Lyndon Johnson put in a full day as
President. He proclaimed Monday a national
day of mourning.

10:53 pm On Camera: The White House, draped in
WHITE HOUSE black. Several lights are burning.

VAN HEFLIN reads Walt Whitman's poem to
Lincoln, "O Captain! My Captain!"

1:02 am SERMONETTE
WNBC-TV ONLY MEMORIAM

THE NATIONAL ANTHEM

Sunday, Nov. 24, 1963

8:08 am
WASHINGTON,
D.C.

MUELLER: The first item on President Johnson's agenda today is an intelligence briefing on the Vietnam situation. . . . Several hundred people have already gathered outside the Capitol.

8:10 am
WHITE HOUSE

VANOCUR: President Johnson may change his plans and go first to St. Mark's Episcopal Church for early services, then to the White House for the intelligence briefing on Vietnam.

8:12 am
WASHINGTON,
D.C.

MUELLER: The President worked for two hours after midnight last night.

MUELLER reads the order of protocol for the cortege, which will be led by Major Gen. Philip Wehle.

8:15 am
NEW YORK

Film: Philadelphia street scenes; people watching TV sets, praying in churches; lowering of the flag at Independence Hall to half-staff.

REP. WILLIAM GREEN (D-Pa.): A heartbreaking shock. . . . We have lost a great friend.

Film: Theaters closed; businesses closed— with explanatory notes scrawled in windows.

◄ Film: President Kennedy's trip to Philadelphia, July 4, 1962, for the Army-Navy game. The President crosses the field at halftime; a man runs up to him, within arm's length, and is pulled away by Secret Service men.

8:29 am
PHILADELPHIA
(WRCV-TV)

Film: The flag-lowering ceremony at the Philadelphia Navy Yard.

Film: Flag-lowering ceremony at Fort Dix, N. J.; memorial service at Valley Forge ("A heartbreaking sorrow has caused a solemn silence to fall upon us."); singing of "Hail to the Chief" by the Independence Hall Choir; Msgr. Charles W. Minaugh, Archdiocese of Philadelphia, speaking from Valley Forge.

9:02 am
HYANNIS PORT

DAVID JAMES: Sen. Edward Kennedy and Mrs. Rose Kennedy are attending mass today at St. Francis Xavier in Boston.

Sunday, Nov. 24, 1963

9:06 am
WASHINGTON, D.C.

MUELLER: Pope Paul has spoken from the Papal Chapel on the death of John F. Kennedy. Queen Frederika of Greece and French President Charles de Gaulle have already boarded planes for Washington. About 2,000 people are lined up in front of the Capitol now. Most of them are young people.

9:07 am
WHITE HOUSE

VANOCUR outlines the President's plans for today.

9:08 am
WASHINGTON, D.C.

Film: The selection of the grave site at Arlington Cemetery.

MUELLER: President Kennedy will be the second President to be buried in Arlington Cemetery.

Film: The Rotunda in the Capitol.

9:17 am
CATHOLIC TV CENTER BOSTON

On Camera: Cardinal Cushing presiding over a pontifical mass.

CARDINAL CUSHING: The world stands helpless at the death. . . . Unprecedented sorrow. . . . Millions lament in a silence which will never again be broken.

10:05 am
NEW YORK

BLAIR: Cardinal Cushing will fly tomorrow to Washington to lead the solemn pontifical mass at St. Matthew's Cathedral. Rev. Charles Chris observed a brief eulogy yesterday at Memorial Church, Harvard Yard, Cambridge, Mass. The Harvard-Yale football game was canceled. All Harvard deeply mourned the death of John F. Kennedy.

STATION IDENTIFICATION

Senator Edward M. Kennedy and mother

10:10 am
WASHINGTON, D.C.

MUELLER: Officials at Arlington are preparing the grave of John F. Kennedy. Joseph F. Kennedy will not attend the funeral of his son.

10:16 am
WHITE HOUSE

VANOCUR: At 3 pm today, President Johnson will receive an intelligence briefing on Vietnam at his home. He will deliver his State of the Union message next Wednesday.

10:18 am
WASHINGTON, D.C.

MUELLER: The news from Dallas is that Gov. Connally is better today.

ABEL: Tomorrow will mark one of the largest assemblages of foreign dignitaries ever seen in Washington. Queen Frederika of Greece and Charles de Gaulle are en route to the capital.

MUELLER: President Johnson will meet with Mrs. Kennedy some time today at the White House. Robert Abernethy reports that the Rotunda is ready for the casket.

10:24 am
NEW YORK

BAPTIST HOUR CHOIR, Fort Worth, Tex., sings a medley of hymns as a tribute to John Kennedy. The selections: "Of Thee I Sing"; "Faith of our Fathers"; and "O God Our Help in Ages Past."

BLAIR: Before the war, when his father was ambassador, John Kennedy spent a great deal of time in London. This morning, in Westminster Abbey, Archdeacon Edward Carpenter delivered his eulogy to the late President.

VIA RELAY SATELLITE FROM LONDON

Tape: Archdeacon Edward Carpenter's eulogy. The Westminster Abbey Choir sings "The Battle Hymn of the Republic."

BLAIR: We pause briefly now for a moment of reflection.

STATION IDENTIFICATION

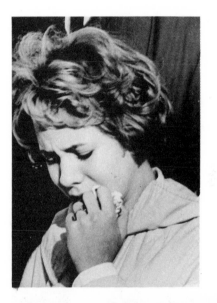

11:05 am
WASHINGTON, D.C.

MUELLER: President Johnson is on his way to services at St. John's now. He will not appear at the White House until after the cortege.

11:06 am
WHITE HOUSE

VANOCUR: The business of state will not be conducted in the White House until Mrs. Kennedy has had time to get her affairs in order.

11:09 am
WASHINGTON, D.C.

MUELLER: A private mass is due to start in a few minutes in the East Room of the White House. Mrs. Kennedy and members of the Kennedy family will attend. A 21-gun salute will honor the late President today. An Honor Guard of servicemen will act as pallbearers in the cortege.

West Point

U.S.A.

Rome: Cardinal Spellman blesses symbolic coffin

Moscow

Tokyo

11:14 am NEW YORK **BLAIR:** The communist news agency in Red China has issued a critical statement on President Johnson. Previously, they had reported the death of Kennedy without comment.

BLAIR introduces tributes from representatives of various faiths.

DR. DAVID C. REED (Minister of Madison Ave. Presbyterian Church): Nobody thinks of this as an accident. . . . It is an accumulation of hatred and bigotry. . . . The church stands for the opposite of hate, but at times like this, words of sweetness and light are not enough.

BLAIR: There was not a single candle to be had in St. Patrick's Cathedral Friday. . . . Friday was also the beginning of the Jewish Holy Days.

DR. LOUIS FINKELSTEIN (Chancellor of the Jewish Theological Seminary): John F. Kennedy lived a martyr's life. He died a martyr's death. The head of the leading state of the world, working for the peace of mankind, was cut down in the midst of his labors.

MSGR. TIMOTHY A. FLYNN (Archdiocese of N. Y.): The death of John F. Kennedy was a great tragedy. . . . We will never know the measure of greatness he would have achieved.

ST. VLADIMIR'S CHOIR, under the direction of David Dillett, sings a medley of hymns.

BLAIR: President Kennedy set a pattern in culture, too. He was equally at home with all the arts. Not all the music he liked was "longhair." One of his favorite tunes was "Greensleeves."

12 noon **RYAN:** One hour from now the body of John Fitzgerald Kennedy will be taken to the Capitol Building. President Johnson, his wife and children are attending church services at St. John's Episcopal Church in Washington.

Sunday, Nov. 24, 1963

12:05 pm
DALLAS
POLICE HDQ.
PETTIT: We are standing in the basement corridor where Lee Oswald will pass through momentarily. Extraordinary security precautions have been taken for the prisoner.

12:07 pm
DALLAS
COUNTY JAIL
MURPHY: I am here with Bill Decker, Sheriff of Dallas County. We are expecting word any moment as to when Oswald will be moved.

12:08 pm
WHITE HOUSE
VANOCUR: The body of the late President will be moved in less than an hour. President Johnson was given an intelligence briefing on Vietnam by CIA Director John McCone; a meeting will be held today at 3:00 pm. . . . Attendance at St. Matthew's Cathedral tomorrow will be by invitation only.

12:13 pm
PENNSYLVANIA
AVENUE
GORALSKI: The temperature is 46°. Crowds of mourners are quietly gathering. The police are wearing mourning clothes. The traffic is heavy.

12:14 pm
CAPITOL
SCHERER: A line four blocks long and four abreast is waiting to view the catafalque in the Rotunda.

12:20 pm
BASEMENT
OF DALLAS
CITY JAIL
On Camera: The start of the transfer of Lee Harvey Oswald from Dallas City Jail to Dallas County Jail. The cameras are trained on Oswald, the accused assassin of President Kennedy. He is flanked by detectives, moving toward the ramp where an armored car is waiting to effect the transfer. Suddenly, out of the lower right corner of the screen, a man wearing a hat lunges forward, his back to the camera. A shot rings out. Oswald gasps, grabs his side and starts to fall.

PETTIT: He's been shot! He's been shot! He's been shot! Lee Oswald has been shot! There's a man with a gun. There's absolute panic, absolute panic here in the basement of the Dallas Police Headquarters. Detectives have their guns drawn. Oswald has been shot. There's no question about it. Oswald has been shot. Pandemonium has broken loose here in the basement of Dallas Police Headquarters.

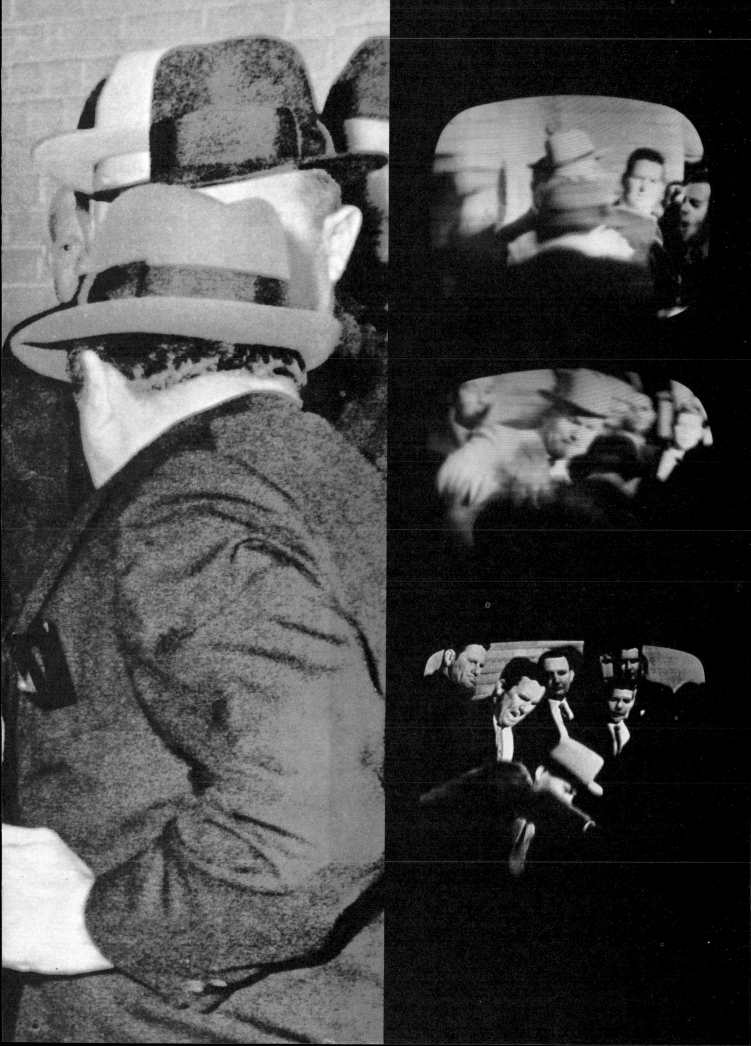

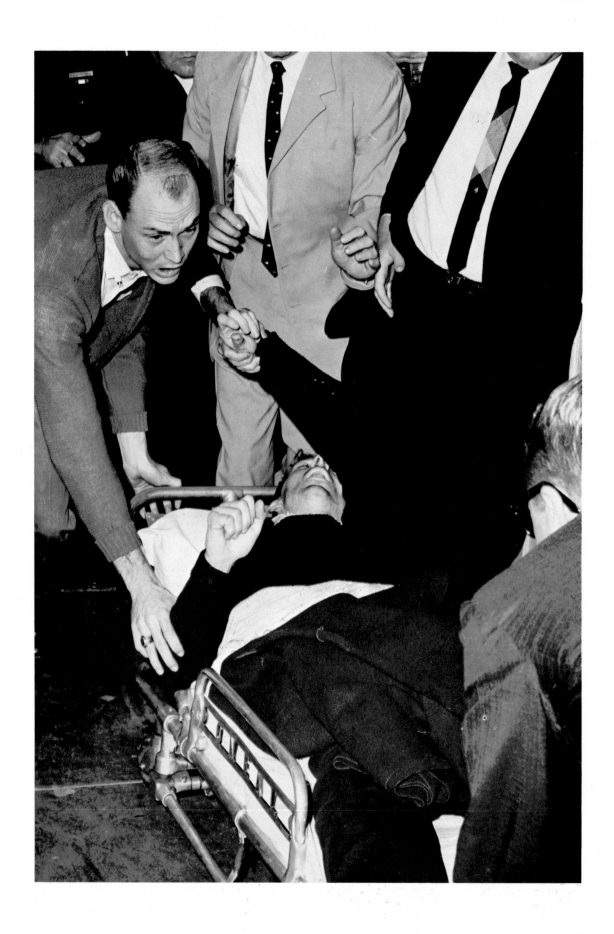

On Camera: Someone in the crowd tells Pettit that the man who shot Oswald was well dressed, in a brown coat and hat, and gave the appearance of being a detective. The ambulance arrives as police are clearing the area.

PETTIT: The police recognized the man. He is known locally, and owns a gambling casino in Dallas.

On Camera: Lying on a stretcher, Oswald is placed in an ambulance.

PETTIT: Oswald will be taken to Parkland Hospital—the same hospital where the mortally wounded President was taken. . . . The man who shot Oswald is known locally. He is in the custody of the Dallas police.

Tape Repeat: The shooting of Lee Harvey Oswald.

PETTIT: The reports are that the man who shot Oswald came out of a green car parked outside the Dallas jail. He had no difficulty whatsoever entering the basement, though the area was supposedly under heavy guard.

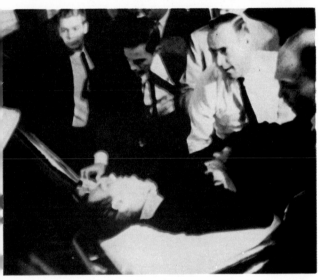

PETTIT interviews a policeman who states that Oswald's assailant is a resident of Dallas, whose name cannot be released at this time. After the shooting, the man was immediately disarmed and subdued by police.

PETTIT gives his eyewitness account of the shooting of Oswald.

12:42 pm
NEW YORK
McGEE: We will replay the tape of this bizarre shooting in slow motion.

Tape Repeat: The Oswald shooting—in slow motion.

McGEE: The man has been identified as Jack Ruby—a nightclub owner in Dallas. Oswald arrived at the hospital about the same time Mrs. Connally arrived to visit her husband, who is recovering from wounds inflicted by an

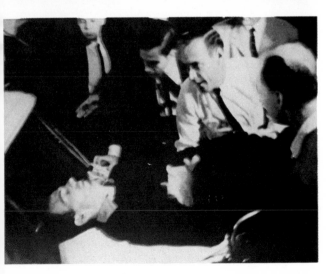

Sunday, Nov. 24, 1963

assassin—to all indications, Oswald himself.
Mrs. Connally was making her first public
statement as the ambulance arrived.
Oswald's head reportedly was lolling from
side to side.

STATION IDENTIFICATION

12:50 pm
WHITE HOUSE

On Camera: President Kennedy's body leaves
the White House for the Capitol Rotunda.

On Camera: The caisson which will bear
President Kennedy's body passes under the
White House portico. Directly behind him is
a single black horse whose stirrups face in
opposite directions, indicating the fallen
leader will never ride him again.
The caisson waits in position. The cadence
is set at 100 steps per minute.

McGEE (voice over): Oswald is in critical
condition at Parkland Hospital.

On Camera: A military Honor Guard appears
at the door, bearing the flag-draped casket
that contains the body of the late President.
The Honor Guard proceeds down the White
House steps, followed by Mrs. Jacqueline
Kennedy, her two children, and Robert
Kennedy, who enter a car to follow the
caisson to the Capitol Rotunda. President and
Mrs. Johnson enter the second car of the
procession. The caisson begins to move.
Muffled drums are heard. Shown entering
cars at the White House are Mrs. Robert
Kennedy and her children; Mr. and Mrs.
Stephen Smith, brother-in-law and sister
of the late President; and others.

PENNSYLVANIA
AVENUE

The procession advances toward the Capitol
—first the caisson, followed by the Honor
Guard; then the riderless horse; the
Presidential flag; additional Honor Guard
units; members of the clergy; the drums;
and the cars of the dignitaries. The
procession turns onto Pennsylvania Avenue,
approaching the Senate wing of the Capitol
building. Numerous people are waiting to
pay their last respects to the President; after

the brief ceremonies, the public will be admitted to the Rotunda. It is a young crowd. Most of the people are in their twenties. The procession halts at the Capitol. The Honor Guard removes the straps binding the casket to the caisson.

Present arms. The U.S. Navy band plays "Hail to the Chief." The guns fire a salute. The Navy Band plays the "Navy Hymn" as the Honor Guard lifts the flag-draped casket from the caisson and slowly proceeds up the Capitol steps into the Rotunda, followed by the Navy man holding the Presidential flag, and Mrs. Kennedy and her children. Inside the Rotunda, the Honor Guard carries the casket to the catafalque, sets it down and departs, making way for a second Honor Guard, which takes up a position around the casket. The casket has been roped off. Foreign dignitaries, members of Congress, and the Kennedy family are present in the Rotunda. The ceremonies begin.

SEN. MIKE MANSFIELD: There was a sound of laughter; in a moment, it was no more. And she took a ring from her finger and placed it in his hands. There was a wit in a man neither young nor old, but a wit full of an old man's wisdom and of a child's wisdom, and then, in a moment, it was no more. And so she took a ring from her finger and placed it in his hands. There was a man marked with the scars of his love of country, a body active with the surge of life far, far from spent, and, in a moment, it was no more. There was a father with a little boy, a little girl, and a joy of each in the other. In a moment it was no more. There was a husband who asked much, and out of the giving and the asking wove with a woman what could not be broken in life, and in a moment it was no more. And so she took a ring from her finger and placed it in his hands, and kissed him and closed the lid of a coffin. A piece of each of us died at that

moment. Yet in death he gave of himself to us. He gave us of a good heart from which the laughter came. He gave us of a profound wit, from which a great leadership emerged. He gave us of a kindness and a strength fused into a human courage to seek peace without fear. He gave us of his love that we too, in turn, might give. He gave that we might give of ourselves, what we might give to one another until there would be no room, no room at all, for the bigotry, the hatred, prejudice and the arrogance which converged in that moment of horror to strike him down. In leaving us these gifts, John Fitzgerald Kennedy, President of the United States, leaves us. Will we take them, Mr. President? Will we have now the sense and the responsibility and the courage to take them?

CHIEF JUSTICE EARL WARREN: There are few events in our national life that unite Americans and so touch the heart of all of us as the passing of a President of the United States. There is nothing that adds shock to our sadness as the assassination of our leader, chosen as he is to embody the ideals of our people, the faith we have in our institutions and our belief in the fatherhood of God and the brotherhood of man. Such misfortunes have befallen the nation on other occasions, but never more shockingly than two days ago. We are saddened; we are stunned; we are perplexed. John F. Kennedy, a great and good President, the friend of all men of good will, a believer in the dignity and equality of all human beings, has been snatched from our midst by the bullet of an assassin. What a price we pay for fanaticism! If we really love this country, if we truly love justice and mercy, if we fervently want to make this nation better for those who are to follow us, we can at least abjure the hatred that consumes people, the false accusations that divide us and the bitterness that begets violence. Our nation is bereaved.

The whole world is poorer because of his loss. But we can all be better Americans because John Fitzgerald Kennedy has passed our way, because he has been our chosen leader at a time in history when his character, his vision and his quiet courage have enabled him to chart for us a safe course through the shoals of treacherous seas that encompass the world. And now that he is relieved of the almost superhuman burdens we imposed on him, may he rest in peace.

REP. JOHN McCORMACK: As we gather here today, bowed in grief, the heartfelt sympathy of the members of the Congress and of our people are extended to Mrs. Jacqueline Kennedy and to Ambassador and Mrs. Joseph Kennedy and their loved ones. Their deep grief is also self-shared by countless millions of persons throughout the world, considered a personal tragedy, as if one had lost a beloved member of his own immediate family. While this is an occasion of deep sorrow, it should also be one of dedication. We must have the determination to unite and carry on the spirit of John Fitzgerald Kennedy for a strengthened America and a future world of peace.

On Camera: President Lyndon Baines Johnson places a wreath at the head of the flag-draped coffin, pauses, bows his head, and then returns to stand with Mrs. Johnson and members of their family. Taking the hand of her daughter Caroline, Mrs. Kennedy walks slowly to the catafalque, kneels, and kisses the flag-draped coffin. At her side, Caroline presses a white-gloved hand to the casket. The Kennedy family files out of the Rotunda. Outside the Capitol building, President and Mrs. Johnson shake hands and speak briefly with Mrs. Jacqueline Kennedy and Robert Kennedy.

McGEE: (voice over): Lee Harvey Oswald died at 2:07 pm today after being shot by Jack Ruby in the Dallas City jail.

Sunday, Nov. 24, 1963

2:27 pm
WHITE HOUSE
On Camera: President Johnson arrives at the White House.

2:28 pm
CAPITOL
On Camera: The area outside the Capitol. Lines of people are waiting to enter the Rotunda to pay their last respects to President Kennedy. Inside the Rotunda, people are moving past the flag-draped coffin. The Honor Guard changes.

SCHERER: The changing of the Honor Guard will take place every half hour.

On Camera: Flowers from the immediate family and from President Johnson are placed near the casket. The camera remains fixed on the Rotunda as people continue to file through.

3:11 pm ABERNETHY: The surge of people toward the Capitol building is creating a serious problem. Some people have been waiting ten to twelve hours.

SCHERER: Others who have lain in state in the Capitol include Sen. Robert A. Taft, as well as the Unknown Soldiers of World War II and the Korean War.

3:34 pm HARVARD GLEE CLUB (audio only) performs 15th century music as the camera continues to show mourners passing by the casket.

STATION IDENTIFICATION

3:45 pm
NEW YORK
McGEE: Lee Oswald was shot at 12:17 EST. Fifteen minutes later he was taken to the emergency room in Parkland Hospital— the same hospital President Kennedy was taken to. Heart massage failed, and Oswald died at 2:07 pm. Jack Ruby, the man who shot Oswald, is a Dallas nightclub owner and is well known to the police.

RYAN: Oswald's chest was opened for heart massage. . . . Jack Ruby is about 50 years old and owns two nightclubs in Dallas— strip-tease joints. His attorney has received two death threats. The U.S. government will establish federal jurisdiction over the case.

McGEE: Lee Harvey Oswald died 48 hours after the President—in the same hospital and the same emergency room. It is a bizarre story—utterly incredible. Oswald had refused the Dallas Bar Association's attorney. Many Dallas lawyers refused to take his case, stating that to do so would ruin their careers. Several lawyers offered to defend Ruby.

4:03 pm
CAPITOL

On Camera: The viewing of the casket by the public.

DICKERSON: Rich and poor alike are on line. The Vice President of Argentina went in with the crowd.

4:07 pm
WASHINGTON, D.C.

ABEL: Among the dignitaries coming from abroad are Prime Minister Alec Douglas-Home and Prince Philip of Great Britain; President Eamon de Valera of Ireland; Prime Minister Hayato Ikeda of Japan; Prince Bernhard of the Netherlands. The Republic of Israel has declared a national mourning period. Madame Pandit of India is also coming.

4:13 pm
DULLES INTERNATIONAL AIRPORT, WASHINGTON, D.C.

NEWMAN: Mexico's Foreign Minister, Manuel Tello, has just arrived.

SEÑOR TELLO: This is an occasion to pay tribute to a great statesman. . . . Mexico is grieved by the tragedy.

4:15 pm
WASHINGTON, D.C.

ABEL: Madame Nhu has sent a very bitter message to Mrs. Kennedy stating that anything that happens in Vietnam will find its counterpart in the U.S. Madame Nhu said in the message that she found it ironic that a communist murdered President Kennedy, because the troubles in her country are also caused by the communists.

4:17 pm
WHITE HOUSE

VANOCUR: Ambassador to Vietnam Henry Cabot Lodge had a luncheon engagement set for today with President Kennedy. He has reported to President Johnson. Ambassador Lodge was Richard Nixon's running mate in 1960. He believes the war in South Vietnam is going well. . . . It is doubtful that Mrs. Kennedy will see the telegram from Madame

107

Sunday, Nov. 24, 1963

Nhu. . . . Everyone is marveling at Mrs. Kennedy's composure; as one observer put it, she has been "a Trojan throughout it all."

4:20 pm
WASHINGTON, D.C.

MUELLER: Mrs. Kennedy will continue to undergo her ordeal tomorrow as she walks behind the caisson bearing her late husband's body from the White House to St. Matthew's Cathedral.

4:21 pm
HYANNIS PORT

DAVID JANE: Mrs. Rose Kennedy, mother of the late President, and Sen. Edward Kennedy are boarding the plane "The Caroline" with security forces.

SEN. KENNEDY: We would like to express our appreciation for the outpouring of sympathy, and thank all the people who have been so kind.

JANE speaks with a friend of the Kennedy family as the plane warms up. The family friend calls Mrs. Rose Kennedy "a remarkable woman." Mr. Joseph Kennedy, the President's father, will remain in the care of his niece, Ann Gargan, who has been tending him since his stroke several years ago. Father John Cavanaugh, of Notre Dame, will also be with Mr. Kennedy during the funeral. The family will take Thanksgiving Dinner together.

4:28 pm
NEW YORK

McGEE: In 1953-1954, Jack Ruby, the man who killed Lee Oswald, was charged with carrying a weapon. He was in trouble with the authorities in 1957 and 1959 for violating liquor ordinances, but he has never been convicted of a felony.

STATION IDENTIFICATION

McGEE: There have been various reactions around the country to Ruby's shooting of Oswald. Some people believe Ruby "should be given a medal." Others think that even if Oswald was guilty, Ruby had no right to kill him. There are those who believe Oswald "got what he deserved," and others who think Ruby's action was that of a gangster—an outrage to justice that compounds the tragedy. Ruby's defense attorney says that Ruby is a fine man who admired the President.

4:40 pm
NEW YORK

McGEE: Lee Oswald died without ever confessing. . . . Jack Ruby's real name is Jack Rubenstein. The remark "I can take care of him" has been falsely attributed to Ruby. . . . Ruby was fond of animals. He never associated with "the ladies," and is not married. It is reported that after hearing of the President's death, Ruby walked around in circles saying, "Oh, that poor family." He was known to the police as a flamboyant character, one who liked to be in on police press conferences and other official matters.

4:44 pm
DULLES INTERNATIONAL AIRPORT

ABEL (voice over) identifies some of the people arriving. Dean Rusk is seen shaking hands with a group of French military officers. He is waiting to greet Prime Minister Ikeda of Japan.

ABEL: Each dignitary to arrive must get the "red carpet treatment."

On Camera: Under Secretary of State Roger Hilsman, with Dean Rusk. A group of Africans are waiting to greet their leaders. Japanese Prime Minister Ikeda arrives, and goes with Rusk and Hilsman to a waiting car.

4:55 pm
WASHINGTON, D.C.

ABEL: President Johnson has been welcoming delegations from 50 states. President de Gaulle is about 25 minutes late in arriving.

4:57 pm
NEW YORK

McGEE: When Jack Ruby shot Lee Oswald, there were cheers. . . . Doctors in Parkland Hospital were unable to save Oswald. A detective in the crowd tried to stop Ruby from shooting Oswald but couldn't reach him in time. Oswald saw the gun. He knew he was going to be shot. The Department of Justice has sent an investigator to Dallas.

4:59 pm
DALLAS POLICE HDQ.

PETTIT: Jack Ruby is being led out of the questioning room—through the same door that Oswald passed. Reporters are crowding around. . . . Dallas is a city of incredible ironies.

Sunday, Nov. 24, 1963

5:00 pm
NEW YORK
McGEE: The UN has suspended all meetings tomorrow.

5:18 pm
CAPITOL
DICKERSON: It is possible that no President will ever again ride in an open car. It was Secret Service man Rufus Youngblood who jumped into the car with President Johnson, covering him with his body after President Kennedy was shot.

On Camera: The Capitol building, lights ablaze.
MUELLER: The mass tomorrow will be a low mass.

5:24 pm
DULLES
INTERNATIONAL
AIRPORT
NEWMAN (voice over): President Charles de Gaulle has arrived, and is standing with Secretary of State Dean Rusk. He is shaking hands with the representatives of the African nations. With de Gaulle is Maurice Couve de Murville, the Foreign Minister of France. De Gaulle will not make a statement. He will stay at the French Embassy in Washington.
ABEL (voice over): Eulogies will be delivered all over the world in honor of the late President. Books of condolence have been opened in American embassies around the world. . . . The crowds are still passing through the Rotunda.

5:35 pm
NEW YORK
McGEE interviews Roy Wilkins, Executive Secretary of the NAACP, who speaks of the sorrowful reaction of American Negroes to the President's death.

5:42 pm
CAPITOL
SCHERER (voice over): Many who pass the coffin are kneeling briefly in prayer. . . . The Honor Guard changes every 30 minutes.

5:48 pm
WHITE HOUSE
VANOCUR: After the funeral and burial, Mrs. Kennedy will receive the heads of state from 3 to 3:30 pm. President Johnson will receive the same group from 5 to 5:30 pm.

6:00 pm
LOS ANGELES
MEMORIAL
STADIUM
On Camera: A memorial service for President Kennedy, produced in cooperation with the Freedom Foundation of Valley Forge.
The National Anthem. Invocation. Reading

of President Eisenhower's statement on the assassination. "Requiem," by Gabriel Fauré, performed by the Roger Wagner Chorale and Orchestra. Address by Dr. Franklin Murphy, Chancellor of U.C.L.A. ("As our President gave leadership, we must assume this leadership that his death shall not be in vain. . . .") "Largo," by George Frederick Handel, performed by the Los Angeles Philharmonic Orchestra. "Requiem," by Johannes Brahms, performed by the Los Angeles Philharmonic Orchestra. "Battle Hymn of the Republic," performed by the Herman Methodist Choir. "Requiem," by Giuseppe Verdi, sung by Mary Costa. Lorne Green reads excerpts from President Kennedy's Inaugural Address. Capt. Jeremiah J. Rodell, U.S. Air Force Chaplain, offers a prayer for John F. Kennedy's soul and for the nation. The Navy Hymn. Taps.

7:10 pm
WASHINGTON, D.C.

Tape: "The Power of the Presidency," a round-table discussion of the problems of Presidential succession, with Sen. Eugene J. McCarthy (D-Minn.), historian Sidney Hyman and political analyst William S. White. Martin Agronsky moderates.

McCARTHY: Historians take the long view. . . . We cannot anticipate what will happen.

HYMAN: We never know about a President until he gets into office. Some men do not seem capable until the job is upon them.

WHITE: Men make events. The ultimate test of power is their ability to act with inner strength, to make quick and dangerous decisions without fear—as in President Truman's decision to send troops to Korea.

McCARTHY: For the President, minor issues are cut away. He can see what his task is.

WHITE: There's a paradox to politics that causes men to have their finest hour at moments of tragedy. And it is at these times that the nation attains true union and spiritual strength.

Sunday, Nov. 24, 1963

HYMAN: Yes, a sort of national discipline sets in. Whereas Congress tends to show up badly when things are going well, in serious crises they unite, and serious men take command. . . . The President is the chief political leader. I don't like the title "Chief Executive."

McCARTHY: The problem of the Presidency is that the white charger and the pale horse of death may look the same. . . . There's no Gallup Poll to help a President decide the important questions.

HYMAN: The Constitution provides for the separation of powers, and for the tenure of the President. He cannot be turned out of office except by impeachment.

McCARTHY: The President is also leader of his party. . . . He often acts best in a crisis.

WHITE: Johnson said in 1960 that he could think of no man who was really "fit" to be President. Every President does as well as he can, with the help of his advisers. He is subject to the forces of history. Mr. Truman's preparation for the office was nil. Roosevelt never told him anything; he didn't even know about the atom bomb project. Mr. Kennedy, on the other hand, brought Lyndon Johnson in on every one of his decisions.

McCARTHY: It is difficult for a President to choose his Cabinet. It is hard to find people you can trust.

Berlin, 1961

WHITE: For his Cabinet, Kennedy selected people he didn't even know, and nearly all of them were older than himself. . . . President Johnson is a truly national figure. He has a deep feeling for the nation as a nation. His strength is in drawing opposing factions together, and in persuading people to compromise. His capacity for persuasion is incredible.

McCARTHY: He gives you the impression that nothing would make him happier than if you changed your opinion to his.

There is a tendency for lawmakers to give the successor what they might not have given the predecessor. They try to expiate their guilt by doing more for the successor. In the present case, this principle may turn out to apply to civil rights.

HYMAN: Succeeding to the Presidency emancipates Johnson from his territorial base.

WHITE: Johnson was more than consulted under the Kennedy administration—he was active in all decisions. He had a cordial relationship with President Kennedy.

McCARTHY: Even as Vice President, Lyndon Johnson was no longer a regional man. . . . In the hill country where Johnson comes from, when they speak about "the war," they mean the Mexican War. . . . But during the Korean War, Johnson did a lot for the Mexican-Americans who fought there. There is no intolerance in Lyndon Johnson In fact, his position is somewhat in advance of most Senate liberals.

WHITE: Johnson has a long record in international affairs. Our allies will trust him; he is truly the "alter ego" of the late President.

HYMAN: When Harry Hopkins represented the U.S., he was received by kings and queens. It is not the man that counts so much as the power represented. The new President is not known in all countries, but he has worked with many allied leaders, and he represents the power of the U.S.

McCARTHY: And he's not alone. He represents the ideals of the West. I don't see our power diminishing abroad.

WHITE: The problems of the White House are always hanging over the President's head.

McCARTHY: And all these same questions came up when Truman succeeded to the Presidency.

STATION IDENTIFICATION

Berlin, 1961

Sunday, Nov. 24, 1963

8:08 pm
NEW YORK

McGEE: Pierre Salinger reports that President Johnson has requested the White House staff to remain. . . . The war in South Vietnam against the Vietcong communist guerrillas continues. Four Americans were captured today. . . . The delegates to the Vatican Council called for Christian unity. . . . The staff of the Soviet Union has been requested to leave the Congo. . . . Jack Ruby says he "couldn't help" shooting Oswald. The Justice Department will continue to investigate the assassination. . . . John Masefield, poet laureate of England, has saluted President Kennedy in a poem.

8:18 pm
CAPITOL

ABERNETHY (voice over): Two hundred thousand people are still outside the Capitol waiting to view the casket. More are coming every minute, and it is getting colder. Many of the mourners are children. The police are keeping the line in motion.

8:24 pm
NEW YORK

McGEE: Mary Ryan, a distant relative of President Kennedy, is coming from Ireland to be at the funeral.

8:25 pm
WASHINGTON, D.C.

Tape: King Baudouin and Paul-Henri Spaak of Belgium pose for photographs with Dean Rusk at Dulles International Airport.

ABEL: At the Capitol, two soldiers have been assigned to accept the floral tributes and place them outside the Rotunda.

8:30 pm
DULLES INTERNATIONAL AIRPORT

KAPLOW (voice over): That is Chancellor Ludwig Erhard posing for photographers with Dean Rusk.

8:32 pm
WHITE HOUSE

HACKES: Today, President Johnson discussed U.S. policy in Vietnam. He will have a busy day tomorrow as well. He will accompany the body of the President on foot and then, after the mass, he will drive to the burial. In the afternoon, Johnson will receive the heads of state. . . . Secret Service agents have been in on the preparations at St. Matthew's Church. . . . A bishop of the Methodist Church has blamed all the people of the U.S. for Kennedy's death.

| 8:37 pm | MUELLER: Banks will close tomorrow, |
| WASHINGTON, D.C. | and the stock market. |

8:38 pm
DULLES INTERNATIONAL AIRPORT

NEWMAN: Dean Rusk is greeting Dr. Zalam Shazar, President of Israel, and Dr. Avraham Harmon, Israel's Ambassador to the U.S.

8:41 pm
NEW YORK

Film: Interview with Mrs. Mary Ryan, cousin of the late President, in Ireland. She speaks of her memories of his visit, his good faith, his good thoughts for his home. Mrs. Ryan sent a message of condolence to Mrs. Jacqueline Kennedy.

McGEE: Church services in memory of President Kennedy are being held today in cities all over the world: Argyle, Scotland; Rome; New York. A Buddhist service was held in Tokyo. Dean Sayre of the Washington National Cathedral said that any man who has ever hated set the stage for this act. Pope Paul spoke regretfully of the capacity for hatred and evil in the human heart.

8:45 pm
CAPITOL

ABERNETHY (voice over): There is no way to speed the line of people filing by. Everybody seems to want to linger.

Tape: The line of people waiting earlier today to enter the Rotunda.

ABERNETHY: The first people arrived at midnight last night, with blankets. It is, in general, a very young crowd.

On Camera: The procession past the casket continues. The faces of the mourners are grief-stricken. A flag waves at half-staff.

8:58 pm
NEW YORK

McGEE: The city of Dallas has been left in shock—one violent discharge after another. The churches of Dallas hold deeply troubled crowds of people, people searching their souls, groping. . . . Something has happened beyond understanding.

STATION IDENTIFICATION

9:00 pm "THE STRANGE STORY OF LEE OSWALD" —an NBC News Special Report.

RYAN: We would like to reconstruct what is known of this man Oswald.

Irish relatives: Miss Josephine and Mrs. Mary Ryan

Mrs. Ryan

Sunday, Nov. 24, 1963

9:02 pm
DALLAS

MacNEIL: This is not a simple story: Oswald was not a simple man. Though charged with the assassination of President Kennedy, he died—technically—an innocent man. But unless something extraordinary happens —again—history will hold him guilty.... Oswald was born Oct. 18, 1939, in New Orleans, La. His father died before he was born. Subsequently his mother moved with him and two other sons to Fort Worth, Texas. At school, Oswald was bookish, but did not get good marks. At the age of 17 he joined the Marines, and was twice court-martialed, but he did manage to qualify as a sharpshooter. When he was released from the Marines he went to Russia, where he married a beautiful Russian girl. On Oct. 30, 1959, he appeared at the U.S. Embassy in Moscow and said he wanted to renounce his American passport. Two years later he became disillusioned with Russia. He returned to New Orleans and became involved in the Fair Play for Cuba Committee. The FBI says that on March 20 of this year, Oswald, using an alias, purchased a rifle with a telescopic sight from a mail-order firm in Chicago. At the beginning of October, Oswald got a job in the Texas School Book Depository in Dallas. This was a few days after President Kennedy's visit to this city had been announced. On October 14 he rented a small apartment for $8.00 a week, half a mile from the warehouse.

Film: Oswald's landlady calls him "polite and thoughtful."

Photograph: Oswald's apartment.

MacNEIL: On November 21, Oswald got up as usual, but did not return Thursday night. He spent the night in Irving, where his wife and children live.

Film: The Oswald home in Irving; the route to Dallas.

MacNEIL: Friday morning, Oswald takes to work a long slim package wrapped with paper and string. He tells a neighbor it is a window blind.

Film: President and Mrs. Kennedy arriving at Love Field, Dallas. The motorcade drives through the heart of the city.

MacNEIL: It is nearly 12:30 Dallas time.

Film: The motorcade rounds the corner. The President slumps down, and Mrs. Kennedy cradles his head in her lap. People at the scene are panic-stricken.

Film: The interior of the School Book Depository.

MacNEIL: Oswald leaves the building and gets on a bus. He goes two blocks, finds the bus too slow, gets out and enters a taxi. He goes to his rented room.

Film: Mrs. Earlene Roberts, the housekeeper, testifies that Oswald came barging in, grabbed his coat, and went out.

MacNEIL: He runs through the Oak Cliff area.

Film: A woman says she saw a police car stop Oswald. ("Oswald leaned in the window, and when the policeman stepped out, Oswald shot him.") Two men, one a garage attendant, testify to seeing Oswald. A shoe store salesman says that Oswald stopped briefly in the lobby of his store, then walked up the street into a theater. The box-office cashier confirms this.

Film: The inside of the movie theater.

MacNEIL: One hundred years ago, the assassination of Abraham Lincoln took place in a theater, and the chase led from there. In this gruesome 20th-century parallel, the chase ends in a theater. But this pathetic hiding place was no help to Oswald. He narrowly avoided lynching and was jailed.

Tape Repeat: Jack Ruby shoots Oswald.

MacNEIL: Oswald was rushed to the hospital —to the same emergency ward where the President was taken. Ten feet from where the President died, Oswald died.

Oswald home

9:20 pm
NEW YORK

RYAN: Dallas police felt they had learned enough about Oswald to secure a conviction. Let's go back to Friday afternoon, when Oswald was questioned about the murder of the Dallas policeman.

Tape: Oswald is questioned by federal and local officers in the homicide bureau of the Dallas Police Department. Capt. Will Fritz leads the questioning.

RYAN: Shortly after 11 am today, Oswald was formally charged with the murder of Dallas policeman J. D. Tippit and the murder of President John F. Kennedy. Dallas police chief Jesse Curry said today he would have moved Oswald last night, but he had already pledged newsmen that the transfer would not take place until today.

9:22 pm
DALLAS
POLICE HDQ.

PETTIT: It was right here in the basement garage of the Dallas police headquarters that an almost incredible series of events took place at 11:20 this morning. Twenty-four year old Lee Oswald, the accused assassin of President Kennedy, was shot and killed—right on this spot.

9:25 pm
NEW YORK

RYAN: Pettit speaks to Dallas police sergeant Patrick Dean, just after the shooting.

Tape Repeat: Pettit asks Dean how Ruby managed to slip in despite all the strict security precautions.

Photograph: Police photo of Jack Ruby.

Tape Repeat: The activity surrounding the shooting. Oswald is carried on a stretcher to the ambulance.

RYAN: There is no end to the irony and the bizarre twists of this story. . . . The doctors were unable to save Oswald's life. The announcement of his death was made by Dr. Thomas Shires, chief resident in surgery at Parkland Hospital.

Film Repeat: The announcement of Oswald's death.

DR. SHIRES: Lee Oswald died at 1:07 pm

Sunday, Nov. 24, 1963

Dallas time of a gunshot wound. He never regained consciousness.

9:30 pm
NEW ORLEANS
Tape Repeat: Oswald's apartment where he lived with his Russian wife.

JIM KENT interviews Oswald's New Orleans landlady.

LANDLADY: He was very quiet. . . . He had a cute little Russian wife. He didn't work much —read a lot. Once he placed a "Fair Play for Cuba" poster on my screen porch, and I made him take it down. He left very suddenly.

KENT interviews a grocer in Oswald's New Orleans neighborhood.

GROCER: Oswald was a peculiar sort of fellow. Not very friendly.

BERN ROTMAN, WDSU-TV, interviews Ed Vogel, a junior high school classmate of Lee Oswald.

VOGEL: We used to talk about ideas and plans. Once we got in a discussion about weapons, and he told me how he planned to rob a store on Rampart St.—there was a gun in the window. I told him not to do it, because of the burglar alarm.

9:44 pm
NEW YORK
RYAN: And what of Jack Rubenstein, Lee Oswald's murderer? He owns a night club and dance hall in Dallas, and calls himself Jack Ruby. His police record is unspectacular. He had a very high regard for the late President.

9:45 pm
LOS ANGELES
Tape: Neal interviews Earl Norman, nightclub comic and friend of Jack Ruby.

NORMAN: Ruby's a two-personality man. He's strong and he's not. He's well-built, in good physical condition, able to defend himself. . . . To my knowledge, he had no gangland connections. . . . He did a lot of good things. . . .

Tape: Neal interviews Nelson Saul, a boyhood friend of Ruby's who has been in contact with him ever since they met.

118

SAUL: A group of very prominent people in Beverly Hills are spearheading a movement to set up a defense for Sparky—that's how we called Jack. I'm in the bail bond business, and I'm going to try to get bail set for him. There's a lot involved in this shooting.

9:54 pm
DALLAS
MURPHY interviews the wife of the slain police officer, J. D. Tippit. She appears on camera with her children.

MRS. TIPPIT: We were told the news by the police department. . . . I don't know how I will manage.

ALLEN TIPPIT (the oldest son): My father always said he wanted me to be something other than a policeman.

MURPHY: The mayor of Dallas has asked the people of the city to come to their senses.

Film: Jack Ruby is taken into custody by the Dallas police.

Film: A review of Ruby's past. Ruby's sister appears on the film, as well as his attorney, who calls Jack Ruby "a law-abiding citizen."

PETTIT interviews Tammy True, a performer in Jack Ruby's club.

TAMMY TRUE: Jack closed the club yesterday. He was extremely emotional over the death of the President.

PETTIT: All of this is so bizarre. Dallas needs to calm down. Questions remain. What is going to happen to Jack Ruby? And what is the evidence against Lee Oswald?

10:05 pm
WASHINGTON, D.C.
VANOCUR: The Justice Department says that the Oswald case is not closed, and they will not allow the Dallas police department to close it. . . . It was bad practice in any case to permit anyone entrance to the basement of the Dallas city jail without a pass.

STATION IDENTIFICATION

10:10 pm
CAPITOL
SCHERER: Peter Lawford, brother-in-law of the late President, has just entered the Rotunda. . . . Mrs. Jacqueline Kennedy

reappeared in the Rotunda tonight, about 9 pm, with Robert Kennedy. They went unnoticed up the stairs.

RASH: Mrs. Kennedy knelt beside the catafalque and touched the flag-draped coffin. She and Robert Kennedy then started toward the limousine. Mrs. Kennedy appeared to change her mind about riding, and they set off across the darkened Capitol plaza. Near First and Constitution Avenues they met a group of nuns, and Mrs. Kennedy stopped to talk with them. Finally, in heavy traffic, Mrs. Kennedy and Robert Kennedy stepped into the official limousine, which had been following them. The entire walk lasted about 15 minutes.

SCHERER: That is Eunice Shriver, the President's sister. . . . Out of respect, the crowds are not thronging around any members of the Kennedy family who are appearing tonight.

In the Rotunda

10:20 pm
DULLES INTERNATIONAL AIRPORT
ABEL: A British airliner has just arrived. Dean Rusk is greeting Harold Wilson, Prime Minister Douglas-Home, the Duke of Edinburgh, and Sir David Ormsby-Gore.

10:34 pm
WHITE HOUSE
HACKES: Mrs. Kennedy has spent another day of mourning with her children. At the end of the 30-day period, Mrs. Kennedy, it is reported, will remain in Washington. She visited the Rotunda again this evening, and seems to be steeling herself for the ordeal tomorrow. After the funeral services, she will hold a brief reception for foreign dignitaries.

10:38 pm
NEW YORK
McGEE: The Dallas police force has declared the Oswald case closed. The Justice Department, however, refuses to accept this.

10:39 pm
DALLAS
Tape: Press conference held by Henry Wade, District Attorney of Dallas, to make public the evidence against Oswald.

WADE: A number of witnesses saw someone with a gun in the window of the School Book Depository. The gun that was used to murder the President was purchased from a mail-order house in Chicago by a man using an assumed name—the same name found in the wallet belonging to Oswald. Witnesses have testified to seeing him after the assassination. They saw him stop and reload his gun, and enter the theater. His fingerprints were found on the rifle. Paraffin tests showed that he had fired a rifle recently. Our office has not closed the investigation, as there is no concrete evidence—but there is no doubt in our minds that Oswald was the assassin.

10:52 pm
WASHINGTON, D.C.

MUELLER: President Johnson hopes to clear up his papers early tonight and get home.

Tape Repeat: Rev. Martin Luther King's statement.

REV. KING: President Johnson has made it clear that he is committed to civil rights generally and to the Civil Rights Bill in particular.

MUELLER: Because 75 high-speed aircraft will salute the President's grave, air traffic has been cleared for the funeral tomorrow.

10:55 pm
WASHINGTON NATIONAL AIRPORT

JOHN GLENN, upon arrival, says that his plane was held up in Texas by a bomb scare. No bomb was found aboard.

10:56 pm
CAPITOL

Tape: President Eamon de Valera of Ireland passes by the casket.

SCHERER: Even though de Valera is very old, and virtually blind, he insisted on making the trip. . . . The guard is being changed now. It changes every thirty minutes.

11:03 pm
NEW YORK

McGEE: Last night, in an abrupt and unprecedented departure from its format of satirical material, the BBC-TV program, "That Was The Week That Was," presented a tribute to President Kennedy.

11:04 pm

Tape: The Saturday, Nov. 23, broadcast of "That Was The Week That Was," BBC-TV, London.

DAVID FROST: It was the least likely thing to happen in the whole world. . . . If anyone else

Outside the Capitol

Sunday, Nov. 24, 1963

had died—Sir Winston Churchill, de Gaulle, Khrushchev—we could have understood.

AL MANCINI: One cannot believe that such a rich, happy, talented family could have so much bad luck. Brother Joe killed in the war . . . sister Rosemary born a mental defective, and sister Kathleen dead in an air crash.

LANCE PERCIVAL: He was the first Western politician in 30 years to make politics a respectable profession.

FROST: Even in death, it seems, we are not equal. Death is not the great leveler. Death reveals the eminent.

MILLICENT MARTIN sings a special song in tribute to John F. Kennedy.

ROBERT LANG: Once again we are reminded that no man is an island and the bell that tolls in Dallas tolls for us all. . . . His death prompts us to remember with Montaigne that sit we never so high upon a stool, yet sit we but upon our own tails. . . .

DAME SYBIL THORNDIKE recites a "Tribute to Jackie."

BERNARD LEVIN: A few hours before he died, President Kennedy had taken time out of his crowded program to look in on a birthday celebration in Dallas for John Nance Garner. Garner, who was 95 yesterday, was Roosevelt's first Vice President. . . . It was he Lyndon Johnson went to for advice when offered the Vice Presidency by Kennedy.

STATION IDENTIFICATION

11:30 pm **Tape Repeat:** The funeral cortege bearing the body of the late President from the White House to the Capitol Rotunda.

12:35 am **On Camera:** Continuing coverage of the
CAPITOL crowds passing the casket and paying last respects to the late President. The music in the background is Beethoven's 7th Symphony, second movement—a dirge.

1:00 am Changing of the Guard.

1:30 am Changing of the Guard.

1:40 am HOLLIS WRIGHT: Washington police announced that mourners were lined up for three miles, five abreast. The size of the crowd has increased with time.

2:00 am Changing of the Guard.

2:03 am WRIGHT: By midnight, over 100,000 people had filed by the flag-draped casket, although the weather dropped to 38°. The crowds are so large, Washington police are afraid that not all will have an opportunity to view the casket.

2:30 am Changing of the Guard.

2:35 am WRIGHT: The crowd now stretches 13 blocks out and 13 blocks back. Some people have been in line for seven and a half hours. Our coverage will continue throughout the night. The "Today" show will start broadcasting at 7 am.

3:00 am Changing of the Guard.

3:07 am WRIGHT: Jersey Joe Walcott, ex-heavyweight champion of the world, just filed past the coffin.

3:15 am WRIGHT: One hundred twenty thousand people have now filed past. The temperature is at freezing.

STATION IDENTIFICATION

3:30 am Changing of the Guard.

3:52 am WRIGHT: Police estimate that 250,000 people will file past the bier before the Rotunda's Changing of the Guard.

4:00 am Changing of the Guard.

4:52 am STATION IDENTIFICATION

5:00 am Changing of the Guard.

5:30 am Changing of the Guard.

5:46 am WRIGHT: Eighty-five thousand additional people will be able to get in. Police are trying to discourage others from joining the line.

6:00 am Changing of the Guard.

6:30 am Changing of the Guard.

Monday, Nov. 25, 1963

7:11 am
ST. MATTHEW'S CATHEDRAL

BLAIR: I am standing across the street from St. Matthew's Cathedral, the church in which the funeral mass for the late President will be said. The church became a cathedral in 1947. Its doors are now draped in black, and people are entering for early masses. Richard Cardinal Cushing will celebrate the low mass, with 1200 invited guests attending. A high mass is one sung by the priest, with other priests present at the altar as deacon and sub deacon. A low mass is intoned rather than sung, and acolytes assist instead of priests. Music is permitted at a low mass. The low mass was requested by the Kennedy family.

7:16 am
WHITE HOUSE

VANOCUR: Mrs. Kennedy will go to the Capitol and then return to the White House, where she will walk on foot behind the caisson to the cathedral, along with members of the Kennedy family, President Johnson, and foreign dignitaries. Today is also the birthday of John-John, the three-year-old son of the late President.

7:37 am
CAPITOL

WALTERS: The young men of the Honor Guard are relieved every half hour, and average four hours of sleep. These same men accompanied the President every time he went in and out of Washington or attended state functions. They had special rehearsals Friday afternoon. The oldest is 37, the youngest 19.

7:42 am
ST. MATTHEW'S CATHEDRAL

BLAIR: This church is not beautiful on the outside, but the interior contains many lovely mosaics and adornments.

7:44 am
WHITE HOUSE

VANOCUR: When Mrs. Kennedy walks behind the caisson in the funeral procession, it will be the first time a First Lady has ever done so.

7:46 am
WASHINGTON, D.C.

SEN. LEVERETT SALTONSTALL (R-Mass.): There are appropriations bills pending in Congress which should be dealt with quickly in order to give President Johnson an

126

opportunity to get acclimated to his new position.

SEN. MIKE MONRONEY (D-Okla.): I agree with Sen. Saltonstall. It is much better to work on these bills than to be idle. Routine work should continue; Congress should not close down for a mourning period. . . . There are many steps before a bill gets to the floor of the Senate.

SEN. SALTONSTALL: Johnson's great talent is for accomplishing the possible; he doesn't try the impossible. The Presidency is a lonely job, but President Johnson understands human nature and will be able to get out of people what he needs.

SEN. MONRONEY: A President needs about six months to get established.

SEN. SALTONSTALL: President Johnson comes more fully equipped with knowledge of Presidential problems than any man before him. He has a reputation as a man able to effect compromises.

SEN. MONRONEY: No man gets 100% of his goal. President Johnson understands the built-in difficulty of the Democratic Party, the division between rural and city groups.

SEN. SALTONSTALL: The President's role is adjustment rather than compromise. The country draws together at a time of tragedy by natural instinct. When Truman ascended to the Presidency he said, "If you want to help me, pray for me."

8:15 am
WHITE HOUSE
VANOCUR: In two and a half hours the body will be taken to the White House, from which point the funeral cortege will proceed to the cathedral. Last night, Mrs. Kennedy and Robert Kennedy returned to the Capitol to visit the casket again. After leaving the Rotunda, they walked a bit. People recognized them and doffed their hats in respect.

8:18 am
WASHINGTON, D.C.
REP. HALE BOGGS (D-La.): I think it is unwise to make any suggestions about the adjournment of Congress at this time.

Although the nation is in mourning, there are decisions to be made by the new President. All speculation about Congress' going home is premature.

REP. JOHN LINDSAY (R-NY): I wasn't aware that Rep. Halleck had made the suggestion to adjourn. Although I am a close friend of the Kennedys, I think it's important for us to stay on the job. The U.S. Congress can't recess or adjourn; we must all pull together. We must wait to hear what the new President will tell us. There are routine bills pending.

REP. BOGGS: The Kennedy children were at the Rotunda yesterday. Little John-John was restless, so he was taken down the hall to Speaker McCormack's office. He saw some small flags on the desk. When he was given one, he asked for another for his father.

8:38 am
CAPITOL

WALTERS: Many of the people who came here brought their children. They wanted them to remember the death of President Kennedy.

8:41 am
ST. MATTHEW'S CATHEDRAL

BLAIR: Many people have attended early masses this morning. At 9 am the church will be cleared. Several hundred people are waiting on the street. A purple velvet catafalque was just taken in. The President's casket will rest on it during the ceremonies.

8:44 am
WHITE HOUSE

VANOCUR: Mrs. Kennedy and Attorney General Robert Kennedy will go to the

Capitol, return to the White House, and then walk to the cathedral. . . . We can recall typical Monday mornings at the White House. . . . The staff would usually be a little late. The President would be late, too, returning from a weekend at Cape Cod.

8:47 am
WASHINGTON, D.C.

AGRONSKY interviews Sen. Thruston Morton (R-Ky.) and Sen. Abraham Ribicoff (D-Conn.).

AGRONSKY: Sen. Ribicoff, as a former Cabinet member, could you evaluate the difference between Kennedy and Johnson? The difference, so to speak, between Boston and Austin.

Monday, Nov. 25, 1963

SEN. RIBICOFF: At Cabinet meetings President Kennedy and Vice President Johnson always sat opposite each other. Kennedy had a great deal of respect for Johnson, and Johnson for Kennedy. Vice President Johnson always had a lot to contribute. His thinking was deep and sound. Lyndon Johnson is the best qualified Vice President ever to ascend to the Presidency. The nation is indeed fortunate.

SEN. MORTON: I was in the Senate and the House with both Kennedy and Johnson, and I had an office across from Jack Kennedy when he was a Senator. We are lucky that, in this hour of misfortune, a man with vast experience has become President. When Franklin Roosevelt died, Harry Truman knew nothing at all about the atomic bomb project. There was also a problem of armed service morale. . . . Lyndon Johnson has been tempered in the hot cauldron of American politics.

SEN. RIBICOFF: Johnson comes from a vastly different background from Kennedy—but American genius molds men across the entire sweep of this country. The Congress of the U.S. is a crucible of discussion and understanding. No one is more dedicated to the Kennedy programs than Lyndon Johnson.

8:55 am
ARLINGTON NATIONAL CEMETERY

AGRONSKY (voice over): An Honor Guard is already standing at the waiting grave.

9:00 am
WASHINGTON, D.C.

SEN. RIBICOFF: Kennedy, a man of patrician background, had a deep feeling for the poor. Johnson, a cattleman, a farmer, a Southerner, feels as strongly as Kennedy did about Negro rights.

9:05 am
ST. MATTHEW'S CATHEDRAL

BLAIR: When police ordered the crowd to move away from the front of the cathedral, they did so without complaining. . . . The interior of the cathedral is decorated with many examples of Renaissance art. . . . Secret Service men are checking the area thoroughly. The cathedral is one-half mile from the White House. The procession will come here from the White House on foot.

9:10 am
CAPITOL

On Camera: People waiting for the casket to be removed.

9:12 am
WASHINGTON, D.C.

DOWNS: These past few days have been days of madness. A Chicago man committed suicide when he heard of the President's death. The thin films of reason and sanity have been scratched. Chief Justice Warren had warned about the dangers of extremism.

AGRONSKY: I hope the country will learn from these events about the danger of hate. . . . Services for Dallas policeman Tippit will be held today. He was the officer shot by Lee Oswald. Texans have donated thousands of dollars to Tippit's widow. . . . A bill will be introduced in Congress to make it a federal crime to kill, assault or threaten the President of the U.S. Lincoln's assassins were tried by a military court. Assassination is an isolated sort of madness. Out of 36 Presidents, four have been assassinated. . . . The riderless horse used in the funeral cortege was presented by Pakistan to Mrs. Kennedy. He was not trained for crowds and did not behave well yesterday.

9:21 am
CAPITOL

AGRONSKY (voice over): The casket is still in place in the Rotunda, attended by the Honor Guard. It will be removed about 9:30 am.

ST. MATTHEW'S
CATHEDRAL

AGRONSKY (voice over): The composer Mozart was buried in a pauper's grave in Vienna, after the world broke the heart of a genius. A martyr dies in vain if he does not inspire others. Americans <u>must</u> remember what John Kennedy stood for. His funeral will be the most solemn wake in history, infused with all the reverence a sorrowing world can provide. When Oswald was killed, a woman was heard to cry out, "Good, I'm glad he's dead." This is an orgy of guilt, anger, hate. Any system of government will work when things are going well, but it's the system that survives a crisis that counts.

131

9:30 am RYAN (voice over from NY): People came
CAPITOL to pay respects to the late President all
through the night. . . . Cardinal Cushing will
officiate at the funeral ceremonies. Mrs.
Kennedy is expected to receive guests from
3 to 3:30 this afternoon. . . . Members of the
Cabinet are now arriving to pay their last
respects to the late President. Only a few
simple floral tributes surround the plain
bronze, flag-draped casket. Speaker of the
House John W. McCormack is standing
near the casket.

BRINKLEY (voice over from Washington
studio): Speaker McCormack is greeting the
Cabinet members now as they come to pay
their respects to the late President. At last
count, 250,000 people had passed through
the Rotunda, and there are some 50,000 still
waiting outside. The Constitution makes
Speaker McCormack next in line for the
Presidency. After him is Sen. Carl Hayden
of Arizona, President pro tempore of the
Senate. This line of succession was provided
by a Constitutional amendment during
the Truman administration.

9:51 am BRINKLEY (voice over): The Rotunda has
CAPITOL been closed to the public since 9 am.

SCHERER (voice over) outlines the order
for the procession.

ABERNETHY (voice over): The members of
the Cabinet are now viewing the casket. The
death watch is changed every 30 minutes,
and is changing right now. The buzzer you
hear in the background is the one that
summons the Senate into session. There will
be a brief meeting this morning to pass a
resolution of sympathy for the Kennedy
family. That is Adlai Stevenson shaking
hands with Congressional officials waiting at
the entrance of the Rotunda. Judge Sarah
Hughes is also present.

ABERNETHY (voice over): The day is very
bright, warmer than yesterday. The Capitol

Monday, Nov. 25, 1963

doors are now closed, and the Honor Guard is
at attention. A military auto is passing.
The Honor Guard now goes into parade rest,
awaiting the arrival of Mrs. Kennedy and
the Attorney General.

HUNTLEY (voice over): This is the final hour.
Shortly, the body of the late President will be
taken from the Capitol building. All through
the night, thousands of Americans passed
through the Rotunda to pay respects to
the late President.

10:14 am
WHITE HOUSE
MUELLER (voice over): Mrs. Kennedy is
expected to emerge from the White House
any minute with the Attorney General.

GORALSKI (voice over): Dignitaries will be
joining the processional to St. Matthew's
Cathedral for low mass. Mrs. Kennedy and
members of the family will proceed alone to
the Capitol. Mrs. Evelyn Lincoln, the late
President's secretary, has just arrived.
The motorcade has begun to pull up to the
front door of the White House. A Secret
Service agent is inside waiting for Mrs.
Kennedy. Traffic has been momentarily
diverted. Everything is silent.

MUELLER (voice over): All attention is now
focused on the portico of the White House.
Everyone awaits Mrs. Kennedy. These will be
her final hours in public for at least 30 days.

10:22 am
CAPITOL
BRINKLEY (voice over): All is in readiness for
the arrival of Mrs. Kennedy and the
Kennedy family.

10:23 am
WHITE HOUSE
BRINKLEY (voice over): Mrs. Kennedy has
just stepped out from the White House, and
is waiting to enter the limousine. Attorney
General Robert Kennedy is coming down the
steps behind her with the Kennedy children.
He is dressed in a morning coat. We can
also see Mrs. Stephen Smith and Sargent
Shriver, and Prince and Princess Radziwill.

GORALSKI (voice over): The cars are now
pulling away from the White House.
Mrs. Kennedy and Robert and Edward
Kennedy are in the first car.

Prince Philip

Monday, Nov. 25, 1963

10:26 am
PENNSYLVANIA
AVENUE

On Camera: Scenes of the procession. Crowds line the streets.

10:30 am
CAPITOL

HUNTLEY (voice over): The number of young people in the crowd is large, and they are not here for a lark. Seven limousines are carrying the Kennedy family.

10:34 am
PENNSYLVANIA
AVENUE

BRINKLEY: The procession is continuing toward the Capitol. In the first car are Mrs. Kennedy, Robert Kennedy, Ted Kennedy and one of the children—believed to be Caroline.

10:36 am
CAPITOL

HUNTLEY (voice over): The cars are now turning into the Capitol plaza. We don't know whether John Jr. is being brought to the ceremony. Yesterday he injected a note of poignancy while in the office of Speaker McCormack. During the ceremony in the Rotunda he grew restless, and a Navy aide took him to McCormack's office. There, a staff member gave him a small American flag to play with. John Jr. asked if he could have another one to take to his Daddy.

BRINKLEY (voice over): The cars are now arriving in the plaza in front of the Capitol building. Mrs. Kennedy, flanked by Robert and Ted Kennedy, is getting out of the car. She is walking up the steps of the Capitol. The stamina of this woman through these past three and four days has been indescribable. It has touched the entire nation.

HUNTLEY (voice over): Mrs. Kennedy and the Kennedy brothers are entering the Rotunda. Now they are proceeding to the casket. All three are kneeling before the casket.

BRINKLEY (voice over): They arise from their kneeling position . . . say their blessings . . . and turn out.

HUNTLEY (voice over): They are now leaving the Capitol Rotunda, proceeding down the steps toward the Plaza.

BRINKLEY (voice over): The Honor Guard is removing the casket from the Rotunda.

Mrs. Kennedy and the Kennedy brothers are standing at attention in the plaza.

HUNTLEY (voice over): As the pallbearers proceed down the steps with the casket, the band will play "Hail to the Chief," followed by "O God of Loveliness."

BRINKLEY (voice over): The pallbearers are carrying the casket to the caisson.

HUNTLEY (voice over): Mrs. Kennedy, Robert and Edward get into their car—followed by the family. They will proceed down Capitol Hill, then on to St. Matthew's Cathedral. Two years, ten months and five days ago, a young President and his wife proceeded down this same hill on the day of his Inauguration. The President had trouble with his top hat.

BRINKLEY (voice over): The cortege continues; the Marine Band continues to play. A parade of military men is following the procession.

11:00 am

NEWMAN (voice over): The Marine Band is passing the Apex building, followed by the West Point Cadets. Crowds line the streets. . . . The Navy Band is now passing, playing "Onward Christian Soldiers." The automobiles are approaching the junction of Independence and Pennsylvania Avenues. They will turn soon onto Pennsylvania Avenue. The most insistent note in the parade is the sound of the drum. . . . Now the horse-drawn caisson is moving down Pennsylvania Avenue. Many people are walking along the sidewalks, keeping pace with the funeral cortege. The cortege is nearing 6th Street and Pennsylvania Avenue. Paratroopers and Marines are going by, and a contingent of military commanders. . . . The procession has halted briefly between 6th and 7th St. . . . Now it continues down Pennsylvania Avenue.

BRINKLEY (voice over): There is nothing quite so moving as the sight of horses pulling a wooden wagon. As the nation grows older,

tradition and significance are added to Pennsylvania Avenue. . . . During the Truman administration, a change was made on the official emblem of the U.S. The eagle is now turned toward the olive branch.

HUNTLEY (voice over): The music you hear now is a funeral march by Frederic Chopin. In front of the caisson is a paratrooper outfit from South Vietnam.

BRINKLEY (voice over): The cortege is approaching the White House. It is now on 15th Street and Pennsylvania Avenue.

HUNTLEY (voice over): Somewhere in the procession there is a contingent of troops from Ireland. We have been unable to identify them as yet.

BRINKLEY (voice over): The cortege is now inside the grounds of the White House, approaching the front door of the north portico. This is the last time at the White House for the President.

HUNTLEY (voice over): The members of the Kennedy family are now descending from their cars. There is Mrs. Kennedy . . . Robert Kennedy . . . Ted Kennedy. . . . Behind them are President Johnson, the heads of state, and foreign dignitaries.

BRINKLEY (voice over): Mrs. Kennedy, Ted and Robert are preparing to lead the walking procession to St. Matthew's Cathedral. No First Lady has ever walked in her husband's funeral procession before. Those are the pipes of Ireland you hear in the background. . . . And there are Prince Philip and Charles de Gaulle.

HUNTLEY (voice over): The procession, led by Mrs. Kennedy, Robert Kennedy and Ted Kennedy, is moving from the White House to St. Matthew's Cathedral. We can also see King Baudouin, President de Gaulle, Haile Selassie.

BRINKLEY (voice over): Following them are

former Presidents Eisenhower and Truman, members of Congress and the Joint Chiefs of Staff.

HUNTLEY (voice over): In the funeral procession are 22 Presidents, three reigning monarchs, and delegations from every country.

BRINKLEY (voice over): The procession is just turning right on 17th Street. The Black Watch Pipists can be heard in the background. The burden here on the protocol officer has been tremendous. Protocol has been largely dismissed, possibly violated—but nobody has minded.

HUNTLEY (voice over): Very probably there has been no state funeral to compare with this one, with the possible exception of the funeral for King George V. . . . The cars that follow the walking procession are carrying the children of Robert Kennedy and Sargent Shriver.

BRINKLEY (voice over): The caisson has halted in front of St. Matthew's Cathedral. Because of the small capacity of the church, admission to the funeral is by invitation only. There are Caroline and John Jr., Cardinal Cushing, Archbishop Patrick O'Doyle. . . . Mrs. Kennedy and her children are ascending the steps to the Cathedral.

12 noon
INSIDE ST. MATTHEW'S CATHEDRAL

BRINKLEY (voice over): The dignitaries are entering and being seated. . . . We can hear choir music in the background. Charles de Gaulle is here, King Baudouin, Chancellor Erhard. . . . Mrs. Kennedy and her children are seated in the first pew. People are continuing to enter. There are Mr. and Mrs. Nixon. . . . Outside, the straps are being loosened from the caisson.

On Camera: The funeral service. The Navy Band plays "Hail to the Chief," followed by a hymn, as the Honor Guard removes the casket from the caisson and, led by Cardinal Cushing, bears it up the steps

and into the cathedral. Before actually entering the cathedral, Cardinal Cushing blesses the coffin with holy water. As Cardinal Cushing recites prayers, the procession moves slowly up the aisle of the church. Cardinal Cushing approaches the altar and recites the 129th Psalm. The casket remains in the center aisle. Cardinal Cushing puts on the prayer capes and begins to recite the pontifical low mass. In the background, Luigi Vena sings "Ave Maria." The choir sings, and the bread is consecrated. The celebrant consecrates the wine. The Lord's Prayer is said. Holy Communion follows. Cardinal Cushing recites the Communion Anthem, and invites all to pray. The mass ends. The Most Rev. Philip Hannan, Auxiliary Bishop of Washington, D.C., speaks from the pulpit. He reads passages from the Bible and from Kennedy speeches, concluding with the Inaugural Address. Cardinal Cushing sprinkles holy water on the coffin as all recite "Our Father." At the end of prayers, Cardinal Cushing returns to the altar and changes vestments. The service ends. People move outside.

BRINKLEY (voice over): Cardinal Cushing is speaking with Mrs. Kennedy, Caroline and John Jr. . . . The band has just played "Hail to the Chief" and "Holy God We Praise Thy Name." Now the flag-draped coffin is being carried down the steps of the cathedral, followed by the Presidential flag; then Mrs. Kennedy, Caroline, John Jr.; Robert and Ted Kennedy; other members of the family, including Mrs. Rose Kennedy; President and Mrs. Johnson. . . . The Honor Guard is placing the coffin on the caisson. The President's widow is standing with her children. John Jr. is holding a book, looking at his mother. She takes the book from him and hands it to Caroline. . . . She is whispering to John Jr. . . . He is going

forward. . . . He salutes his father's coffin. . . . Today is John Jr.'s third birthday. . . . The members of the family and the foreign dignitaries are entering the cars which will follow the caisson to John Fitzgerald Kennedy's final resting place in Arlington National Cemetery. There is General de Gaulle; Queen Frederika of Greece; Presidents Truman and Eisenhower; Margaret Truman Daniel. Bells are tolling in the background. . . . The drums have begun to beat, as the cortege begins to move toward Arlington. The caisson is drawn by six gray horses. It is proceeding down Rhode Island Ave. . . . now Connecticut Ave. . . . The band is playing "Onward Christian Soldiers."

DICKERSON (voice over): Now the band is playing Chopin's "Funeral March." The cortege is moving down Connecticut Ave., past the sidewalks lined with mourners. It is a clear, bright, chilly day. There is a great stillness.

ABEL: The car carrying President Johnson is surrounded by Secret Service men.

On Camera: A panoramic view of the cortege.
BRINKLEY (voice over): We are now looking from the Lincoln Memorial down Baker Street at the streets lined with people, as the cortege proceeds toward Arlington National Cemetery. It is now on Constitution Ave. The band is playing "Onward Christian Soldiers." The cortege will soon cross the Potomac River. From this view we can see the Lincoln Memorial. . . . The caisson is now entering upon Memorial Bridge. This bridge, a gift of Italy after World War II, is flanked by two golden horses. Now we can see the headstones in Arlington Cemetery.

HUNTLEY (voice over): We are now panning over the President's last resting place. It is an open area behind the site of the Custis-Lee mansion.

BRINKLEY (voice over): The caisson is expected to reach the grave site a while before the procession. . . . The band is now playing "America, the Beautiful."

2:32 pm

KAPLOW (voice over): The cortege is still a good distance from the grave site. The only other President buried here is William Howard Taft. . . . At the request of Mrs. Jacqueline Kennedy, an "eternal flame" will be placed beside the grave of the late President. . . . The caisson has stopped at the nearest driveway. Despite the thousands present, there are only a few hushed sounds. The members of the Kennedy family are still waiting.

BRINKLEY (voice over): There is to be a wait while the rest of the procession catches up. The U.S. Air Force Bagpipes are playing "The Mist over the Mountain." Mrs. Kennedy, Robert and Ted Kennedy are watching from a nearby limousine as the casket bearing the body of the late President is being removed from the caisson. . . . The military pallbearers are carrying the casket to the gravesite. Only two weeks ago, on Armistice Day, President Kennedy was here at Arlington to pay tribute to the Unknown Soldier. . . . The Irish Guard salutes the casket. . . . Fifty jet planes are flying over the grave site. . . . Now the Kennedy family is being shown to their places around the casket. . . . The flag will now be removed from the coffin.

CARDINAL CUSHING offers the benediction: "Our Father." A 21-gun salute is sounded. Cardinal Cushing continues with prayers, as Mrs. Kennedy and Robert Kennedy advance to the casket. The flag that had draped the casket is folded by the military pallbearers and handed to the Director of Arlington National Cemetery. Cardinal Cushing offers the final benediction. The Director hands the folded flag to Mrs. Kennedy, who, with the flag in one hand, lights the "eternal

flame" that rests on the grave site of her
late husband. She, in turn, hands the lighter
to Robert and Edward Kennedy, who also
light the flame. Mrs. Kennedy and Robert
Kennedy leave the grave site hand-in-hand,
followed by members of the Kennedy family.
Cardinal Cushing is seen comforting the
late President's mother, Mrs. Rose Kennedy.
Mrs. Jacqueline Kennedy stops to speak
with Gen. Maxwell Taylor.

BRINKLEY (voice over): And so on this day,
John F. Kennedy is laid to rest on a sloping
hillside in Virginia. . . . We can see various
members of Congress and their wives. . . . In
the background, the limousines are leaving
for the embassies. . . . This afternoon, at
the White House, Mrs. Kennedy will receive
foreign dignitaries and chiefs of state who
have come from all over the world to
pay their respects to her late husband. . . .
The Soviet people have seen a TV
documentary of the assassination and the
subsequent shooting of Lee Oswald.

HUNTLEY (voice over): The Honor Guard is
leaving the grave site. In the background
we can see the graves of other fallen heroes,
and the Custis-Lee mansion. The shafts of
sunlight through the trees create a lovely
effect. The flame is flickering on the
President's grave. The coffin has not been
lowered.

BRINKLEY (voice over): Mrs. Kennedy has
behaved splendidly. It is almost unbelievable
how she has been able to contain her
sorrow. . . . The casket is now being lowered.
. . . The act that killed the President was
spawned by bigotry and extremism, but it has
had an opposite effect on people here,
drawing them together in the spirit of
tragedy. Waiting to see the President's
casket, people invited others to step ahead of
them in line. If this spirit persists, we
will see a gain out of a loss.

Monday, Nov. 25, 1963

3:38 pm
WHITE HOUSE

VANOCUR (voice over): Officials are arriving to call on Mrs. Kennedy, coming directly from the cemetery to the White House. The Korean delegation has entered, and Prime Minister Ikeda of Japan; Emperor Haile Selassie of Ethiopia; Dr. Hector Escobar Serrano of El Salvador; the Nigerian delegation; Anastas Mikoyan of the Soviet Union; Dr. Ralph Bunche of the UN; U Thant, Secretary General of the UN; the Ghana delegation, with UN Ambassador Alex Quaison-Sackey; President Shazar of Israel; the Vietnamese delegation; the Finnish delegation; the Tunisian delegation, with Foreign Minister Mongi Slim and Habib Bourguiba, Jr.; Mohammed Ali Daar from Somali; Gen. Augustin Munoz Grandes, Vice Premier of Spain, sent by Generalissimo Franco; President Macapagal of the Philippines and Mrs. Macapagal; Dr. Victor Belaunde, UN Ambassador from Peru; the Czech delegation.

NEWMAN (voice over): At the grave, Cardinal Cushing described President Kennedy as "Thy departed servant." Mrs. Kennedy's composure throughout the rush of events these past few days has been remarkable. Hardened reporters were seen weeping. This unutterably sad day is drawing to a close.

STATION IDENTIFICATION

4:10 pm
NEW YORK

RYAN: Officer Tippit was buried today in Dallas, as was Lee Harvey Oswald.

5:10 pm
WASHINGTON, D.C.

MUELLER: Today was John-John's third birthday. . . . The duties of the Presidency go on. At an official reception at the New State Department building, President Johnson is receiving dignitaries from foreign nations.

5:11 pm
NEW STATE DEPT. BLDG.

MUELLER (voice over): There is G. Mennen Williams. . . . Madame Pandit. . . . Secretary of State Dean Rusk has joined the President at the door. The African officials are now entering.

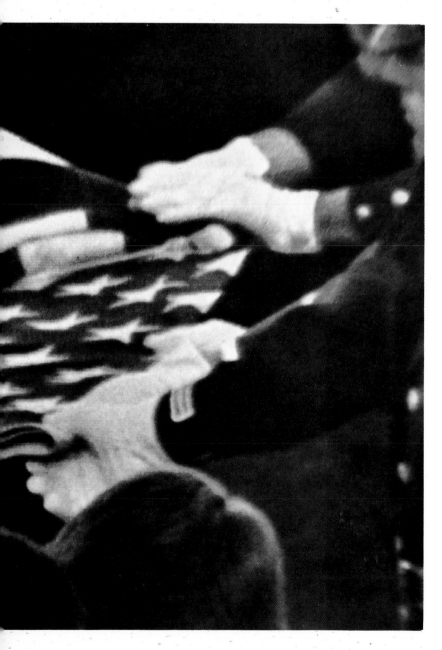

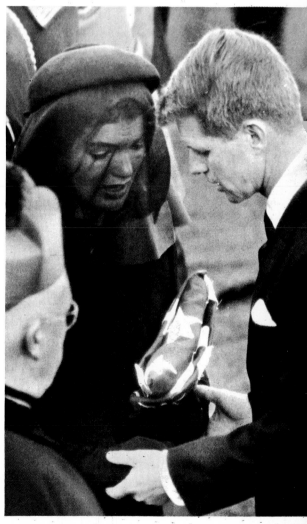

Monday, Nov. 25, 1963

NEWMAN (voice over): The Prime Minister of Turkey is entering. Each head of state was permitted to bring two others with him.

ABEL (voice over): Now we can see President de Valera of Ireland . . . Queen Frederika of Greece . . . Haile Selassie of Ethiopia. Many Africans are arriving. . . . Now an Indonesian group, and the Prime Minister of Japan . . . Lester Pearson, Prime Minister of Canada. . . . This room is a large, comfortable lounge with large chairs and a fireplace. . . . Ralph Bunche, Paul Hoffman, other UN officials . . . King Baudouin of Belgium . . . Paul-Henri Spaak of Belgium. Prince Philip and Prime Minister Douglas-Home have entered and are posing for photographs with President Johnson.

DICKERSON (voice over): During one political campaign, Lyndon Johnson developed a sore hand from shaking hands so often. . . . The delegation from Algeria has arrived . . . followed by the Apostolic Delegate representing Pope Paul. . . . Now West Berlin Mayor Willy Brandt is standing with Johnson. . . . The Prime Minister of Jamaica has arrived . . . Africans from Brazzaville and the Cameroons . . . Princess Beatrix of the Netherlands . . . the Dutch foreign minister . . . the Italian delegation . . . the ambassador from Peru. . . . Lady Bird Johnson, the new First Lady, has just arrived and joined the receiving line. . . . Now the Korean delegation . . . the people from the Ivory Coast . . . Mikoyan from the Soviet Union . . . and Poland's ambassador.

6:15 pm   **HUNTLEY-BRINKLEY NEWS SPECIAL**

WASHINGTON, D.C.   **BRINKLEY:** The burial of President John F. Kennedy ended today in dignity and grandeur. The Kennedy family has now gone into seclusion. After the funeral, Mrs. Kennedy received the heads of state at the White House and President Johnson greeted them at the State Department. It was the greatest turnout of heads of state in the history of the world. The American people flooded into Washington to pay their final respects to the late President.

HUNTLEY: The death of King Edward in England marked the end of the Victorian Era. We hope that with the death of John F. Kennedy another era will end, and we will see the beginning of peace.

Film: President Johnson's reception.

6:40 pm
WASHINGTON, D.C.

HUNTLEY: The U.S. is joined in mourning today by the entire world. In Russia, Mrs. Khrushchev wept. The funeral was telecast by relay satellite. Many warriors in Nairobi wept. Red China was the only country to strike a discordant note.

7:18 pm
WASHINGTON, D.C.

Tape: Carl Sandburg reads a poetic eulogy to President Kennedy.

9:35 pm

"LBJ REPORT NUMBER ONE"
—a biography and evaluation of President Lyndon Baines Johnson.

WHITE HOUSE

LEE DAYTON recaps President Johnson's day today, quoting his statement, "Our whole system of government is on trial."

10:00 pm
WASHINGTON, D.C.

SCHERER: Now that Lyndon Johnson is President, what cooperation can he hope for in the Senate?

SEN. DIRKSEN: We cannot expect a great upheaval. People believe in what they believe in and they always will.

SEN. HUMPHREY: President Johnson will have a good relationship with Congress.

SEN. DIRKSEN: There will be a general rallying around the President.

ABERNETHY, with Rep. Hale Boggs (D-La.) and Rep. Gerald Ford (R-Mich.), discusses the relationship between the President and the House of Representatives. The two Congressmen feel that the members of the House

Monday, Nov. 25, 1963

already have a warm relationship with the new President. He is a big man, they say, and will not shrink from controversy even in an election year.

10:44 pm
ABEL: President Johnson tonight held his first meetings on foreign affairs. There is no reason to think that Johnson will change Kennedy's stand on foreign policy.

10:58 pm
PALM BEACH FLORIDA (WPTV)
H. V. KALTENBORN: We are facing one of the greatest crises of our times. This tragic event will have a profound effect on our people. So far, Americans have stood forth with dignity and integrity. It is inherent in the American character to react the right way at the right time. Throughout these three days, everyone—no matter who—said the right thing. The nation is most fortunate to have a strong man follow a strong man. President Johnson is the type of man we like to see take charge in an emergency.

12:22 am
Tape: Special memorial concert from Constitution Hall, Washington, D.C. Howard Mitchell conducts the Washington Symphony Orchestra.

ORCHESTRA PLAYS "Symphony for the Common Man" by Aaron Copland.

MITCHELL: The last time President and Mrs. Kennedy attended the Washington Symphony, the President requested to hear the "Andante Cantabile" from Tchaikovsky's 5th Symphony.

ORCHESTRA PLAYS "Andante Cantabile" from Symphony #5 by Peter Ilyich Tchaikovsky.

MITCHELL: President Kennedy had a passion for the sea.

ORCHESTRA PLAYS "La Mer" by Claude Debussy.

1:17 am
DAYTON: This concludes NBC's special broadcast schedule covering the death and funeral of John Fitzgerald Kennedy.

On Camera: The Presidential Seal.

NATIONAL ANTHEM

SIGN-OFF

PICTURE CREDITS